Mometrix
TEST PREPARATION

SST®

ntroduction to usiness
xam Secrets tudy Guide

DEAR FUTURE EXAM SUCCESS STORY

First of all, **THANK YOU** for purchasing Mometrix study materials!

Second, congratulations! You are one of the few determined test-takers who are committed to doing whatever it takes to excel on your exam. **You have come to the right place.** We developed these study materials with one goal in mind: to deliver you the information you need in a format that's concise and easy to use.

In addition to optimizing your guide for the content of the test, we've outlined our recommended steps for breaking down the preparation process into small, attainable goals so you can make sure you stay on track.

We've also analyzed the entire test-taking process, identifying the most common pitfalls and showing how you can overcome them and be ready for any curveball the test throws you.

Standardized testing is one of the biggest obstacles on your road to success, which only increases the importance of doing well in the high-pressure, high-stakes environment of test day. Your results on this test could have a significant impact on your future, and this guide provides the information and practical advice to help you achieve your full potential on test day.

Your success is our success

We would love to hear from you! If you would like to share the story of your exam success or if you have any questions or comments in regard to our products, please contact us at **800-673-8175** or **support@mometrix.com**.

Thanks again for your business and we wish you continued success!

Sincerely,
The Mometrix Test Preparation Team

Need more help? Check out our flashcards at:
http://MometrixFlashcards.com/DSST

Written and edited by the Mometrix Exam Secrets Test Prep Team
Printed in the United States of America

TABLE OF CONTENTS

Introduction

Thank you for purchasing this resource! You have made the choice to prepare yourself for a test that could have a huge impact on your future, and this guide is designed to help you be fully ready for test day. Obviously, it's important to have a solid understanding of the test material, but you also need to be prepared for the unique environment and stressors of the test, so that you can perform to the best of your abilities.

For this purpose, the first section that appears in this guide is the **Secret Keys**. We've devoted countless hours to meticulously researching what works and what doesn't, and we've boiled down our findings to the five most impactful steps you can take to improve your performance on the test. We start at the beginning with study planning and move through the preparation process, all the way to the testing strategies that will help you get the most out of what you know when you're finally sitting in front of the test.

We recommend that you start preparing for your test as far in advance as possible. However, if you've bought this guide as a last-minute study resource and only have a few days before your test, we recommend that you skip over the first two Secret Keys since they address a long-term study plan.

If you struggle with **test anxiety**, we strongly encourage you to check out our recommendations for how you can overcome it. Test anxiety is a formidable foe, but it can be beaten, and we want to make sure you have the tools you need to defeat it.

Secret Key #1 – Plan Big, Study Small

There's a lot riding on your performance. If you want to ace this test, you're going to need to keep your skills sharp and the material fresh in your mind. You need a plan that lets you review everything you need to know while still fitting in your schedule. We'll break this strategy down into three categories.

Information Organization

Start with the information you already have: the official test outline. From this, you can make a complete list of all the concepts you need to cover before the test. Organize these concepts into groups that can be studied together, and create a list of any related vocabulary you need to learn so you can brush up on any difficult terms. You'll want to keep this vocabulary list handy once you actually start studying since you may need to add to it along the way.

Time Management

Once you have your set of study concepts, decide how to spread them out over the time you have left before the test. Break your study plan into small, clear goals so you have a manageable task for each day and know exactly what you're doing. Then just focus on one small step at a time. When you manage your time this way, you don't need to spend hours at a time studying. Studying a small block of content for a short period each day helps you retain information better and avoid stressing over how much you have left to do. You can relax knowing that you have a plan to cover everything in time. In order for this strategy to be effective though, you have to start studying early and stick to your schedule. Avoid the exhaustion and futility that comes from last-minute cramming!

Study Environment

The environment you study in has a big impact on your learning. Studying in a coffee shop, while probably more enjoyable, is not likely to be as fruitful as studying in a quiet room. It's important to keep distractions to a minimum. You're only planning to study for a short block of time, so make the most of it. Don't pause to check your phone or get up to find a snack. It's also important to **avoid multitasking**. Research has consistently shown that multitasking will make your studying dramatically less effective. Your study area should also be comfortable and well-lit so you don't have the distraction of straining your eyes or sitting on an uncomfortable chair.

The time of day you study is also important. You want to be rested and alert. Don't wait until just before bedtime. Study when you'll be most likely to comprehend and remember. Even better, if you know what time of day your test will be, set that time aside for study. That way your brain will be used to working on that subject at that specific time and you'll have a better chance of recalling information.

Finally, it can be helpful to team up with others who are studying for the same test. Your actual studying should be done in as isolated an environment as possible, but the work of organizing the information and setting up the study plan can be divided up. In between study sessions, you can discuss with your teammates the concepts that you're all studying and quiz each other on the details. Just be sure that your teammates are as serious about the test as you are. If you find that your study time is being replaced with social time, you might need to find a new team.

Secret Key #2 – Make Your Studying Count

You're devoting a lot of time and effort to preparing for this test, so you want to be absolutely certain it will pay off. This means doing more than just reading the content and hoping you can remember it on test day. It's important to make every minute of study count. There are two main areas you can focus on to make your studying count.

Retention

It doesn't matter how much time you study if you can't remember the material. You need to make sure you are retaining the concepts. To check your retention of the information you're learning, try recalling it at later times with minimal prompting. Try carrying around flashcards and glance at one or two from time to time or ask a friend who's also studying for the test to quiz you.

To enhance your retention, look for ways to put the information into practice so that you can apply it rather than simply recalling it. If you're using the information in practical ways, it will be much easier to remember. Similarly, it helps to solidify a concept in your mind if you're not only reading it to yourself but also explaining it to someone else. Ask a friend to let you teach them about a concept you're a little shaky on (or speak aloud to an imaginary audience if necessary). As you try to summarize, define, give examples, and answer your friend's questions, you'll understand the concepts better and they will stay with you longer. Finally, step back for a big picture view and ask yourself how each piece of information fits with the whole subject. When you link the different concepts together and see them working together as a whole, it's easier to remember the individual components.

Finally, practice showing your work on any multi-step problems, even if you're just studying. Writing out each step you take to solve a problem will help solidify the process in your mind, and you'll be more likely to remember it during the test.

Modality

Modality simply refers to the means or method by which you study. Choosing a study modality that fits your own individual learning style is crucial. No two people learn best in exactly the same way, so it's important to know your strengths and use them to your advantage.

For example, if you learn best by visualization, focus on visualizing a concept in your mind and draw an image or a diagram. Try color-coding your notes, illustrating them, or creating symbols that will trigger your mind to recall a learned concept. If you learn best by hearing or discussing information, find a study partner who learns the same way or read aloud to yourself. Think about how to put the information in your own words. Imagine that you are giving a lecture on the topic and record yourself so you can listen to it later.

For any learning style, flashcards can be helpful. Organize the information so you can take advantage of spare moments to review. Underline key words or phrases. Use different colors for different categories. Mnemonic devices (such as creating a short list in which every item starts with the same letter) can also help with retention. Find what works best for you and use it to store the information in your mind most effectively and easily.

Secret Key #3 – Practice the Right Way

Your success on test day depends not only on how many hours you put into preparing, but also on whether you prepared the right way. It's good to check along the way to see if your studying is paying off. One of the most effective ways to do this is by taking practice tests to evaluate your progress. Practice tests are useful because they show exactly where you need to improve. Every time you take a practice test, pay special attention to these three groups of questions:

- The questions you got wrong
- The questions you had to guess on, even if you guessed right
- The questions you found difficult or slow to work through

This will show you exactly what your weak areas are, and where you need to devote more study time. Ask yourself why each of these questions gave you trouble. Was it because you didn't understand the material? Was it because you didn't remember the vocabulary? Do you need more repetitions on this type of question to build speed and confidence? Dig into those questions and figure out how you can strengthen your weak areas as you go back to review the material.

Additionally, many practice tests have a section explaining the answer choices. It can be tempting to read the explanation and think that you now have a good understanding of the concept. However, an explanation likely only covers part of the question's broader context. Even if the explanation makes perfect sense, **go back and investigate** every concept related to the question until you're positive you have a thorough understanding.

As you go along, keep in mind that the practice test is just that: practice. Memorizing these questions and answers will not be very helpful on the actual test because it is unlikely to have any of the same exact questions. If you only know the right answers to the sample questions, you won't be prepared for the real thing. **Study the concepts** until you understand them fully, and then you'll be able to answer any question that shows up on the test.

It's important to wait on the practice tests until you're ready. If you take a test on your first day of study, you may be overwhelmed by the amount of material covered and how much you need to learn. Work up to it gradually.

On test day, you'll need to be prepared for answering questions, managing your time, and using the test-taking strategies you've learned. It's a lot to balance, like a mental marathon that will have a big impact on your future. Like training for a marathon, you'll need to start slowly and work your way up. When test day arrives, you'll be ready.

Start with the strategies you've read in the first two Secret Keys—plan your course and study in the way that works best for you. If you have time, consider using multiple study resources to get different approaches to the same concepts. It can be helpful to see difficult concepts from more than one angle. Then find a good source for practice tests. Many times, the test website will suggest potential study resources or provide sample tests.

Practice Test Strategy

If you're able to find at least three practice tests, we recommend this strategy:

Untimed and Open-Book Practice

Take the first test with no time constraints and with your notes and study guide handy. Take your time and focus on applying the strategies you've learned.

Timed and Open-Book Practice

Take the second practice test open-book as well, but set a timer and practice pacing yourself to finish in time.

Timed and Closed-Book Practice

Take any other practice tests as if it were test day. Set a timer and put away your study materials. Sit at a table or desk in a quiet room, imagine yourself at the testing center, and answer questions as quickly and accurately as possible.

Keep repeating timed and closed-book tests on a regular basis until you run out of practice tests or it's time for the actual test. Your mind will be ready for the schedule and stress of test day, and you'll be able to focus on recalling the material you've learned.

Secret Key #4 – Pace Yourself

Once you're fully prepared for the material on the test, your biggest challenge on test day will be managing your time. Just knowing that the clock is ticking can make you panic even if you have plenty of time left. Work on pacing yourself so you can build confidence against the time constraints of the exam. Pacing is a difficult skill to master, especially in a high-pressure environment, so **practice is vital**.

Set time expectations for your pace based on how much time is available. For example, if a section has 60 questions and the time limit is 30 minutes, you know you have to average 30 seconds or less per question in order to answer them all. Although 30 seconds is the hard limit, set 25 seconds per question as your goal, so you reserve extra time to spend on harder questions. When you budget extra time for the harder questions, you no longer have any reason to stress when those questions take longer to answer.

Don't let this time expectation distract you from working through the test at a calm, steady pace, but keep it in mind so you don't spend too much time on any one question. Recognize that taking extra time on one question you don't understand may keep you from answering two that you do understand later in the test. If your time limit for a question is up and you're still not sure of the answer, mark it and move on, and come back to it later if the time and the test format allow. If the testing format doesn't allow you to return to earlier questions, just make an educated guess; then put it out of your mind and move on.

On the easier questions, be careful not to rush. It may seem wise to hurry through them so you have more time for the challenging ones, but it's not worth missing one if you know the concept and just didn't take the time to read the question fully. Work efficiently but make sure you understand the question and have looked at all of the answer choices, since more than one may seem right at first.

Even if you're paying attention to the time, you may find yourself a little behind at some point. You should speed up to get back on track, but do so wisely. Don't panic; just take a few seconds less on each question until you're caught up. Don't guess without thinking, but do look through the answer choices and eliminate any you know are wrong. If you can get down to two choices, it is often worthwhile to guess from those. Once you've chosen an answer, move on and don't dwell on any that you skipped or had to hurry through. If a question was taking too long, chances are it was one of the harder ones, so you weren't as likely to get it right anyway.

On the other hand, if you find yourself getting ahead of schedule, it may be beneficial to slow down a little. The more quickly you work, the more likely you are to make a careless mistake that will affect your score. You've budgeted time for each question, so don't be afraid to spend that time. Practice an efficient but careful pace to get the most out of the time you have.

Secret Key #5 – Have a Plan for Guessing

When you're taking the test, you may find yourself stuck on a question. Some of the answer choices seem better than others, but you don't see the one answer choice that is obviously correct. What do you do?

The scenario described above is very common, yet most test takers have not effectively prepared for it. Developing and practicing a plan for guessing may be one of the single most effective uses of your time as you get ready for the exam.

In developing your plan for guessing, there are three questions to address:

- When should you start the guessing process?
- How should you narrow down the choices?
- Which answer should you choose?

When to Start the Guessing Process

Unless your plan for guessing is to select C every time (which, despite its merits, is not what we recommend), you need to leave yourself enough time to apply your answer elimination strategies. Since you have a limited amount of time for each question, that means that if you're going to give yourself the best shot at guessing correctly, you have to decide quickly whether or not you will guess.

Of course, the best-case scenario is that you don't have to guess at all, so first, see if you can answer the question based on your knowledge of the subject and basic reasoning skills. Focus on the key words in the question and try to jog your memory of related topics. Give yourself a chance to bring the knowledge to mind, but once you realize that you don't have (or you can't access) the knowledge you need to answer the question, it's time to start the guessing process.

It's almost always better to start the guessing process too early than too late. It only takes a few seconds to remember something and answer the question from knowledge. Carefully eliminating wrong answer choices takes longer. Plus, going through the process of eliminating answer choices can actually help jog your memory.

Summary: Start the guessing process as soon as you decide that you can't answer the question based on your knowledge.

How to Narrow Down the Choices

The next chapter in this book (**Test-Taking Strategies**) includes a wide range of strategies for how to approach questions and how to look for answer choices to eliminate. You will definitely want to read those carefully, practice them, and figure out which ones work best for you. Here though, we're going to address a mindset rather than a particular strategy.

Your odds of guessing an answer correctly depend on how many options you are choosing from.

Number of options left	5	4	3	2	1
Odds of guessing correctly	20%	25%	33%	50%	100%

You can see from this chart just how valuable it is to be able to eliminate incorrect answers and make an educated guess, but there are two things that many test takers do that cause them to miss out on the benefits of guessing:

- Accidentally eliminating the correct answer
- Selecting an answer based on an impression

We'll look at the first one here, and the second one in the next section.

To avoid accidentally eliminating the correct answer, we recommend a thought exercise called **the $5 challenge**. In this challenge, you only eliminate an answer choice from contention if you are willing to bet $5 on it being wrong. Why $5? Five dollars is a small but not insignificant amount of money. It's an amount you could afford to lose but wouldn't want to throw away. And while losing $5 once might not hurt too much, doing it twenty times will set you back $100. In the same way, each small decision you make—eliminating a choice here, guessing on a question there—won't by itself impact your score very much, but when you put them all together, they can make a big difference. By holding each answer choice elimination decision to a higher standard, you can reduce the risk of accidentally eliminating the correct answer.

The $5 challenge can also be applied in a positive sense: If you are willing to bet $5 that an answer choice *is* correct, go ahead and mark it as correct.

Summary: Only eliminate an answer choice if you are willing to bet $5 that it is wrong.

Which Answer to Choose

You're taking the test. You've run into a hard question and decided you'll have to guess. You've eliminated all the answer choices you're willing to bet $5 on. Now you have to pick an answer. Why do we even need to talk about this? Why can't you just pick whichever one you feel like when the time comes?

The answer to these questions is that if you don't come into the test with a plan, you'll rely on your impression to select an answer choice, and if you do that, you risk falling into a trap. The test writers know that everyone who takes their test will be guessing on some of the questions, so they intentionally write wrong answer choices to seem plausible. You still have to pick an answer though, and if the wrong answer choices are designed to look right, how can you ever be sure that you're not falling for their trap? The best solution we've found to this dilemma is to take the decision out of your hands entirely. Here is the process we recommend:

Once you've eliminated any choices that you are confident (willing to bet $5) are wrong, select the first remaining choice as your answer.

Whether you choose to select the first remaining choice, the second, or the last, the important thing is that you use some preselected standard. Using this approach guarantees that you will not be enticed into selecting an answer choice that looks right, because you are not basing your decision on how the answer choices look.

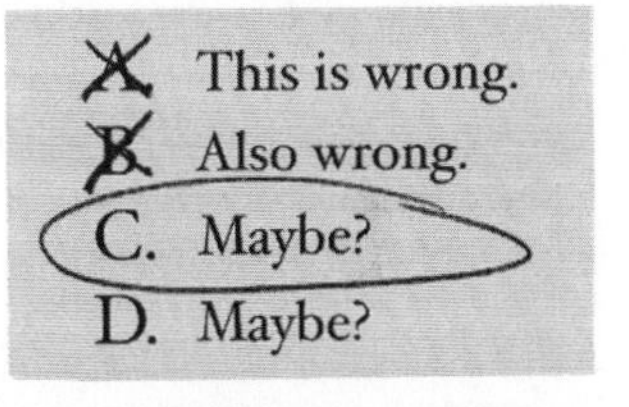

This is not meant to make you question your knowledge. Instead, it is to help you recognize the difference between your knowledge and your impressions. There's a huge difference between thinking an answer is right because of what you know, and thinking an answer is right because it looks or sounds like it should be right.

Summary: To ensure that your selection is appropriately random, make a predetermined selection from among all answer choices you have not eliminated.

Test-Taking Strategies

This section contains a list of test-taking strategies that you may find helpful as you work through the test. By taking what you know and applying logical thought, you can maximize your chances of answering any question correctly!

It is very important to realize that every question is different and every person is different: no single strategy will work on every question, and no single strategy will work for every person. That's why we've included all of them here, so you can try them out and determine which ones work best for different types of questions and which ones work best for you.

Question Strategies

☑ Read Carefully

Read the question and the answer choices carefully. Don't miss the question because you misread the terms. You have plenty of time to read each question thoroughly and make sure you understand what is being asked. Yet a happy medium must be attained, so don't waste too much time. You must read carefully and efficiently.

☑ Contextual Clues

Look for contextual clues. If the question includes a word you are not familiar with, look at the immediate context for some indication of what the word might mean. Contextual clues can often give you all the information you need to decipher the meaning of an unfamiliar word. Even if you can't determine the meaning, you may be able to narrow down the possibilities enough to make a solid guess at the answer to the question.

☑ Prefixes

If you're having trouble with a word in the question or answer choices, try dissecting it. Take advantage of every clue that the word might include. Prefixes can be a huge help. Usually, they allow you to determine a basic meaning. *Pre-* means before, *post-* means after, *pro-* is positive, *de-* is negative. From prefixes, you can get an idea of the general meaning of the word and try to put it into context.

☑ Hedge Words

Watch out for critical hedge words, such as *likely, may, can, often, almost, mostly, usually, generally, rarely,* and *sometimes.* Question writers insert these hedge phrases to cover every possibility. Often an answer choice will be wrong simply because it leaves no room for exception. Be on guard for answer choices that have definitive words such as *exactly* and *always.*

☑ Switchback Words

Stay alert for *switchbacks.* These are the words and phrases frequently used to alert you to shifts in thought. The most common switchback words are *but, although,* and *however.* Others include *nevertheless, on the other hand, even though, while, in spite of, despite,* and *regardless of.* Switchback words are important to catch because they can change the direction of the question or an answer choice.

✓ FACE VALUE

When in doubt, use common sense. Accept the situation in the problem at face value. Don't read too much into it. These problems will not require you to make wild assumptions. If you have to go beyond creativity and warp time or space in order to have an answer choice fit the question, then you should move on and consider the other answer choices. These are normal problems rooted in reality. The applicable relationship or explanation may not be readily apparent, but it is there for you to figure out. Use your common sense to interpret anything that isn't clear.

Answer Choice Strategies

✓ ANSWER SELECTION

The most thorough way to pick an answer choice is to identify and eliminate wrong answers until only one is left, then confirm it is the correct answer. Sometimes an answer choice may immediately seem right, but be careful. The test writers will usually put more than one reasonable answer choice on each question, so take a second to read all of them and make sure that the other choices are not equally obvious. As long as you have time left, it is better to read every answer choice than to pick the first one that looks right without checking the others.

✓ ANSWER CHOICE FAMILIES

An answer choice family consists of two (in rare cases, three) answer choices that are very similar in construction and cannot all be true at the same time. If you see two answer choices that are direct opposites or parallels, one of them is usually the correct answer. For instance, if one answer choice says that quantity *x* increases and another either says that quantity *x* decreases (opposite) or says that quantity *y* increases (parallel), then those answer choices would fall into the same family. An answer choice that doesn't match the construction of the answer choice family is more likely to be incorrect. Most questions will not have answer choice families, but when they do appear, you should be prepared to recognize them.

✓ ELIMINATE ANSWERS

Eliminate answer choices as soon as you realize they are wrong, but make sure you consider all possibilities. If you are eliminating answer choices and realize that the last one you are left with is also wrong, don't panic. Start over and consider each choice again. There may be something you missed the first time that you will realize on the second pass.

✓ AVOID FACT TRAPS

Don't be distracted by an answer choice that is factually true but doesn't answer the question. You are looking for the choice that answers the question. Stay focused on what the question is asking for so you don't accidentally pick an answer that is true but incorrect. Always go back to the question and make sure the answer choice you've selected actually answers the question and is not merely a true statement.

✓ EXTREME STATEMENTS

In general, you should avoid answers that put forth extreme actions as standard practice or proclaim controversial ideas as established fact. An answer choice that states the "process should be used in certain situations, if..." is much more likely to be correct than one that states the "process should be discontinued completely." The first is a calm rational statement and doesn't even make a definitive, uncompromising stance, using a hedge word *if* to provide wiggle room, whereas the second choice is far more extreme.

⊘ Benchmark

As you read through the answer choices and you come across one that seems to answer the question well, mentally select that answer choice. This is not your final answer, but it's the one that will help you evaluate the other answer choices. The one that you selected is your benchmark or standard for judging each of the other answer choices. Every other answer choice must be compared to your benchmark. That choice is correct until proven otherwise by another answer choice beating it. If you find a better answer, then that one becomes your new benchmark. Once you've decided that no other choice answers the question as well as your benchmark, you have your final answer.

⊘ Predict the Answer

Before you even start looking at the answer choices, it is often best to try to predict the answer. When you come up with the answer on your own, it is easier to avoid distractions and traps because you will know exactly what to look for. The right answer choice is unlikely to be word-for-word what you came up with, but it should be a close match. Even if you are confident that you have the right answer, you should still take the time to read each option before moving on.

General Strategies

⊘ Tough Questions

If you are stumped on a problem or it appears too hard or too difficult, don't waste time. Move on! Remember though, if you can quickly check for obviously incorrect answer choices, your chances of guessing correctly are greatly improved. Before you completely give up, at least try to knock out a couple of possible answers. Eliminate what you can and then guess at the remaining answer choices before moving on.

⊘ Check Your Work

Since you will probably not know every term listed and the answer to every question, it is important that you get credit for the ones that you do know. Don't miss any questions through careless mistakes. If at all possible, try to take a second to look back over your answer selection and make sure you've selected the correct answer choice and haven't made a costly careless mistake (such as marking an answer choice that you didn't mean to mark). This quick double check should more than pay for itself in caught mistakes for the time it costs.

⊘ Pace Yourself

It's easy to be overwhelmed when you're looking at a page full of questions; your mind is confused and full of random thoughts, and the clock is ticking down faster than you would like. Calm down and maintain the pace that you have set for yourself. Especially as you get down to the last few minutes of the test, don't let the small numbers on the clock make you panic. As long as you are on track by monitoring your pace, you are guaranteed to have time for each question.

⊘ Don't Rush

It is very easy to make errors when you are in a hurry. Maintaining a fast pace in answering questions is pointless if it makes you miss questions that you would have gotten right otherwise. Test writers like to include distracting information and wrong answers that seem right. Taking a little extra time to avoid careless mistakes can make all the difference in your test score. Find a pace that allows you to be confident in the answers that you select.

✓ KEEP MOVING

Panicking will not help you pass the test, so do your best to stay calm and keep moving. Taking deep breaths and going through the answer elimination steps you practiced can help to break through a stress barrier and keep your pace.

Final Notes

The combination of a solid foundation of content knowledge and the confidence that comes from practicing your plan for applying that knowledge is the key to maximizing your performance on test day. As your foundation of content knowledge is built up and strengthened, you'll find that the strategies included in this chapter become more and more effective in helping you quickly sift through the distractions and traps of the test to isolate the correct answer.

Now that you're preparing to move forward into the test content chapters of this book, be sure to keep your goal in mind. As you read, think about how you will be able to apply this information on the test. If you've already seen sample questions for the test and you have an idea of the question format and style, try to come up with questions of your own that you can answer based on what you're reading. This will give you valuable practice applying your knowledge in the same ways you can expect to on test day.

Good luck and good studying!

Foundations of Business

DUAL TAXATION

Dual taxation is also known as double taxation. One type of dual taxation affects corporations in this manner:

- Profits garnered by the corporation are subject to the corporate income tax
- Plus individual shareholders in the corporation are subject to personal income tax on the dividends paid them by the corporation
- One way around dual taxation is to annually "zero out" the corporation, where the corporation pays its officer(s) a total salary whose sum is equal to the net profits of the corporation. Thus, the taxable income of the corporation is zero, and the only taxes due are the personal taxes owed by the recipient(s)
- Another way to mitigate against dual taxation is to create an "S" corporation (as opposed to a "C" corporation), in which all the income of the corporation is included in the income of the shareholders and is thus subject to being taxed only once

SOLE PROPRIETORSHIP DISADVANTAGES

Sole proprietorship exposes the business owner to significant legal exposure, as he is personally liable for any claims of personal liability or indebtedness incurred by the business.

- Such claims may be made by customers, employees of the business, competitors, or creditors to whom the business is indebted
- Individuals or businesses filing such claims can legitimately pursue all personal assets of the business owner, including bank accounts, real estate, vehicles, and even personal property such as jewelry and household goods
- Real estate jointly owned by a husband and wife, such as a personal residence, may be exempted from claims against one of the spouses; but if both the husband and the wife are involved in the functioning of the business, even these may be in jeopardy

SOLE PROPRIETORSHIP ADVANTAGES

You get to work as your own boss, as opposed to working for an employer.

- It is relatively easy to start up (and to terminate) your business
- Sole proprietorship offers simple tax reporting, in which the profits of the business are taxed as the personal income of the business owner. As a sole proprietorship, the business is subject to no corporate taxes
- The earning potential of a sole proprietor is not limited by an externally imposed fixed salary, depending rather upon the effort the proprietor chooses to put into the business (assuming, of course, that the business is a viable one)
- As a sole proprietor, the business owner himself is responsible for and gets credit for the quality of his product and/or service
- Sole proprietorships are subject to fewer regulatory constraints than other types of corporations

Corporation Protection

Because the corporation itself is the owner of the business, the individual shareholders, directors, and officers of the business are not legally responsible for the debts of the business.

- A creditor does not have the right to seek recovery from these individuals, but, rather, must seek recompense from the assets of the corporation
- However, in the case of fraudulent or negligent acts by agents of the corporation which result in personal harm or loss to an outside party, the corporation will not provide these agents of the corporation with protection from personal liability
- If a creditor has obtained a personal guarantee from the shareholders, this creditor may pursue recompense from the shareholders personally

LLC

Like a regular "C" corporation," a Limited liability corporation (LLC) provides its members with limited protection from personal liability or from debts incurred by the business.

- Unlike a C corporation, an LLC is a "pass-through" entity, meaning that the company's profits (and/or losses) are transferred directly to the members of the LLC, avoiding the double taxation problem incurred by C corporations
- These profits (and/or losses) are then reported on the individual members' tax returns in a manner identical to that employed by sole proprietorships or partnerships

Bankruptcy

The basic features of the four basic types of bankruptcy: Chapter 7, Chapter 11, Chapter 12, and Chapter 13 are the following:

- Under Chapter 7, a debtor seeks the discharge of his debts, otherwise known as "liquidation." No plan for repayment of these debts is necessary, because the assets of the debtor are gathered and sold to repay creditors
- Chapter 11 is often referred to as a "reorganization" bankruptcy, as opposed to liquidation. Here, a bankruptcy plan, generally submitted by any interested creditor(s), identifies how the company's debts are to be repaid and how the company's future operations are to be conducted
- Chapter 12 provides for "family farmers" of "family fishermen" with what the law defines as a "regular annual income" to propose and to implement a plan to pay off all, or a portion, of their debts
- Chapter 13 applies to individual wage earners with regular income, and is often referred to as a "wage earners plan." The specific advantage of Chapter 13 is that it allows individuals to stop foreclosure proceedings on their homes

Conventional ("C") Corporation

Choose an available name which conforms to the rules of the corporation's state of business.

- Appoint the directors who will initially be the officers of the corporation
- File the formal paperwork referred to as the "articles of incorporation" and pay the filing fees determined by the state in which the corporation will be incorporated
- Hold the initial meeting of the corporation's board of directors
- Distribute stock certificates to the shareholders of the corporation

- Acquire whatever licenses and/or permits required by the state of incorporation for the particular type of business done by the corporation
- And contrast the three fundamental types of partnerships

General Partnerships

General partnerships are a partnership formed by two or more persons.

Profits and liabilities are shared equally by the partners, except as described in the partnership agreement.

Limited Partnership

Limited partnership is similar to a general partnership, except that in addition to the general partner(s), there are one or more limited partners, who invest in the company but are neither involved in management of the company nor liable for losses beyond their investment.

Master Partnership

Master limited partnership: A relatively recent type of partnership, in which the business appears similar to a corporation but is taxed like a partnership.

Corporate Mergers

The three types of corporate mergers include the following:

- Vertical merger are two distinct businesses which conduct different phases of a related business join as one entity. For example, a company which produces electric guitar pickups could merge with another company that manufactures electric guitars
- Horizontal merger are two firms in the same industry join forces, enabling the new combined company to diversify or expand upon the existing company's line of products. For example, a clothing manufacturer merges with a designer, resulting in new lines of apparel
- Conglomerate merger is when two firms in unrelated industries (and often in different geographic areas) are joined in order to expand corporate territories and/or to expand a product range.

Unlimited Liability

Unlimited liability is the main disadvantage of sole proprietorship—implies the risk that the losses incurred by the business result in personal losses by the business owner.

- In this case, any debts or damages incurred by the business become the personal debts and damages which are the responsibility the business owner to ameliorate, whether by selling off assets such as bank accounts, real estate (possibly including the business owner's home), or personal property such as jewelry or automobiles
- Also, under unlimited liability, each partner is responsible for the business's losses, even if these losses were caused by one of the business's partners

Limited Liability

Under limited liability, the partners are not responsible for debts or losses incurred by the company above and beyond the value of their investment in the business. Here, personal assets may not be seized to compensate creditors.

ALIEN CORPORATION

Alien Corporation is a company incorporated in a foreign country. The term is occasionally used as a synonym for "foreign corporation," but in the United States, a "foreign corporation" is one that does business in a state or jurisdiction other than the one in which it was incorporated.

DOMESTIC CORPORATION

Domestic Corporation is a US corporation which operates in a state in which it is incorporated (the opposite of a foreign corporation).

FOREIGN CORPORATION

Foreign Corporation in the United States is a corporation registered to do business in a state or jurisdiction other than the one in which it was incorporated. Alternately, a corporation incorporated in a foreign country which is authorized to do business in the United States.

FRANCHISEE ADVANTAGES AND DISADVANTAGES

Franchise advantages are a recognized name with an established franchise, you get instant name recognition.

- Assistance in management and marketing; the franchisor may assist in site selection and in promotion
- The franchisor often provides phone support and e-mail access to assist the franchisee in resolving problems
- Reduced risk of failure
- Historically, independent businesses have a far greater rate of failure than do franchises

PERSONAL OWNERSHIP

Personal ownership is when the franchisee operates essentially as a sole proprietor, though he must adhere to certain defined corporate standards. Disadvantages include:

- Large start-up costs. The cost of starting a franchise for a nationally known operation can run in the hundreds of thousands (and even millions) of dollars
- Being subject to onerous corporate rules. The management directives and imperatives coming down from the franchisor can mitigate against the independence which the franchisee may have sought
- Shared profit. In addition to coming up with the start-up costs, the franchisee may be required to pay to the franchisor a share of the profits or a commission based on gross sales
- Domino effect. If other franchises in the chain fail, a successful franchisee might be forced out of business. Also, the chain might set up other franchises in locations which directly compete with a pre-established franchisee

CLOSED CORPORATION

A closed corporation (also known as a private corporation or a privately held corporation) is one whose stock is not available to the general public but is owned by a few people.

OPEN CORPORATION

An open corporation is one whose shares are traded in the public market and are available to the general public.

Quasi-Public Corporation

A quasi-public corporation is a privately owned company with government backing. A quasi-public corporation has specifically mandated responsibilities to perform services to the public. A quasi-public corporation may issue stock which is available to the general public, but its main duty is to provide the specified services, rather than increase shareholder value.

Article of Incorporation Components

The most common components of an article of incorporation are:

- Corporation name—must be unique in the desired jurisdiction of the person(s) incorporating the company (usually members of the board of directors)
- Whether the corporation is a stock corporation or a nonstock corporation
- Whether the corporation is permanent (perpetual) or for a limited duration
- The purpose of the corporation
- The number of shares the corporation may issue
- The address of the corporation's "registered office"
- Designation and address of the corporation's "registered agent"—the person to whom legal papers to the corporation are to be served
- Minimum capital required by the corporation
- Whether the corporation is "for profit" or "nonprofit"
- The organization and objectives of cooperatives

Corporate Bylaws

Corporate bylaws, also known as a corporate constitution, are the rules establishing how a corporation conducts its internal governance. These rules are established by the board of directors upon establishing the corporation. Among the topics addressed by corporate bylaws are:

- Where the corporation is located
- The date and location of the corporation's annual meetings
- The identification of the corporation's officers
- The duties of the corporation's officers
- How to select officers
- Guidelines as to how stock will be issued

Cooperative

A cooperative is a form of business organization which is equally owned and operated by the people who use its services or who work at it.

- In a cooperative, producers, consumers, and/or workers unite voluntarily in their mutual interest to achieve their common economic, cultural, and social needs through the democratically controlled company
- One objective of cooperatives may be to unite disparate groups, such as owners, employees, managers, and consumers with a business enterprise designed to provide for their common interests
- Another objective may be to enhance the economic power of its members by uniting them in a group, as opposed to their having to fend for themselves as individuals

LEVERAGED BUYOUTS

A leveraged buyout is the takeover of a company or a controlling interest in a company through the significant use of borrowed money, which is used to buy out the interests of the company's stockholders.

- A leveraged buyout may be pursued by employees of the company; by management of the company; or by a group of investors
- Frequently, the assets of the acquired company are used as collateral for the borrowed funds
- A leveraged buyout may be sought by employees of a company who feel there is a good chance that they may lose their jobs
- Or a company's managers may feel that under their leadership the company's performance could be improved
- Finally, a group of investors may feel that the company to be acquired is undervalued and thus offers a good bargain

GOVERNMENT PROPOSALS BIDS

Before you can bid on government proposals, three registrations are needed:

- The Dun & Bradstreet D-U-N-S Number; this is a nine-digit identification number for each physical location of your business. The D-U-N-S Number assignment is free. It is necessary to obtain in order to register with the federal government for contracts or grants. To register, go to http://fedgov.dnb.com
- Register your business as a Central Contractor with the federal government at https://www.bpn.gov/ccr/default.aspx. This is the primary database comprising vendors doing business with the federal government, and registration therein is required by federal acquisitions regulations before a contract can be awarded or a basic agreement can be made
- Click on https://orca.bpn.gov/login.aspx to fill out the Online Representations and Certifications form, which requires additional information about your business and activities

MINORITY-OWNED FIRMS GOVERNMENTAL ASSISTANCE

The Minority Business Development Agency (MBDA) provides capital for Business Development Centers (BDCs) around the country. BDCs were designed to help minority-owned firms begin operations, expand, and develop. The resources available to minority entrepreneurs are:

- Minority Business Enterprise Centers (MBECs)
- Native American Business Enterprise Centers (NABECs)
- Business Resource Centers (BRCs), which address the needs of each firm on an individual basis, offering management and technical assistance throughout the business development process
- Minority Business Opportunity Committees (MBOCs), which coordinate local businesses and federal and state resources to help propel a firm into the marketplace

FEDERAL GOVERNMENT GRANTS

The federal government does not provide grants for starting and expanding businesses, except to nonprofit educational institutes specializing in medicine, scientific research, education, or technology development and to state and local governments (in the form of grants) to assist them with economic development. However, small businesses can get grants through state and local governments, with help from the federal government.

- Specialized business expansion and development, such as expanding child care centers, creating energy-efficient technology, and developing marketing campaigns for tourism, can receive grants from the state, usually in the form of matching funds or in combination with a loan or other financing mechanisms
- Businesses that are not specialized can receive help from both federal and state government agencies in obtaining low-interest loans (http://business.gov/finance/financing/loans/) and venture capital financing (http://business.gov/finance/financing/venture-capital/) from commercial lenders

GOVERNMENT SMALL BUSINESS LOANS

The government does not make loans directly to small businesses or to their owners.

- Instead, the government offers a guaranty to banks and other lenders for capital lent to small businesses
- In other words, it promises to pay some of the loan back in case the business owner defaults, thus reducing the lender's risk
- Business owners who are unqualified for traditional loans still can receive a loan. To get a loan:
    - Ask your local commercial bank or lending institution for a loan
    - Fill out the appropriate forms to apply for a government-backed loan
    - The lender will work with the government as the application works through the system
    - Since there are hundreds of government loans available for small business, find the ones that seem right for you at http://search.business.gov/startLoans.html and organize the documentation that you will need

BUSINESS INCOME TAX FORMS

Whatever form of business you choose (e.g., sole proprietorship, partnership, LLC, C corporation, S corporation) determines which of the various income tax return forms you have to file. There are four basic types of business taxes that the federal government levies:

- Income tax
- Self-employment tax
- Taxes for employers
- Excise taxes

To learn more about these taxes and which forms you would need to file, go to the website of the US Internal Revenue Service:

http://www.irs.gov/businesses/small/index.html?cm_sp=ExternalLink-_-Federal-_-

TREASURY

Each state and local government has its own tax laws and levies taxes on businesses and corporations. Like federal taxes, state tax requirements depend on the legal structure of the business. To see what the requirements are in a particular state, go to: http://www.business.gov/finance/taxes/state.html

Sarbanes-Oxley Act of 2002

The Sarbanes-Oxley Act was enacted in 2002 as a response to a multitude of accounting and corporate scandals, the most notorious of which occurred at Enron, Adelphia, WorldCom, and Tyco International.

- These scandals cost investors billions of dollars when the offending companies' stock dropped precipitously, resulting in a major loss of investor confidence in the securities markets
- The legislation, which does not apply to privately held companies, provides new and enhanced standards and procedures for publicly held companies, including more transparent financial disclosure and more accurate assessment of risk
- The main complaint against Sarbanes-Oxley is that it places undue costs and burdens upon US companies, making them less competitive in world markets

FTC

The principal mission of the FTC is to promote consumer protection and to eliminate harmful business practices.

- The FTC investigates issues raised by consumers, businesses, media reports, or congressional inquiries
- Among the issues investigated by the FTC are allegations of fraud, false advertising, and anticompetitive business practices such as monopolies
- When the FTC determines that one or more of these allegations are factual, among the corrective remedies it might employ is acceptance of voluntary compliance by the offending business, filing of an administrative complaint, or initiation of federal legal action

FNMA

The Federal National Mortgage Association (FNMA), commonly known as Fannie Mae, was founded during the Great Depression but was chartered by Congress in 1968. It is an investor-owned corporation whose purpose is to buy and securitize mortgages, so that institutions have sufficient funds to lend to home buyers.

Federal Home Loan Mortgage Corporation

The Federal Home Loan Mortgage Corporation, often referred to as Freddie Mac, was created in 1979 to compete with Fannie Mae, in order to create a more dynamic and effective secondary mortgage market.

Together, Fannie Mae and Freddie Mac hold roughly half of the twelve trillion dollar mortgage market in the United States.

Glass-Steagall Act

Two separate and distinct US laws compose the Glass-Steagall Act, which was enacted in 1933 in response to the Great Depression.

- The first act was passed in 1932 as an attempt to curb deflation
- The second act, passed in 1933, was designed to resurrect the commercial banking industry
- The main feature of the bill was to protect investors, and to support this effort the act included a prohibition on collaboration between commercial banks and full-service brokerage firms

- The act was repealed in 1999 by the Gramm-Leach-Biley Act, eliminating provisions of Glass-Steagall which prohibited bank holding companies from owning other financial companies
- Many observers blame its repeal for the wave of wild speculation in the subprime mortgage market, which resulted in the global financial crisis which began in 2007

Federal Reserve

The Federal Reserve ("Fed") is the central banking system of the United States.

- It was created in response to the Great Depression in order to prevent such a financial crisis from occurring in the future
- It is not privately owned and is not a for-profit enterprise
- Its mission is to influence the conditions which it believes will lead to fuller employment, stable prices, and reasonable interest rates
- The Fed sets the nation's monetary policy, supervises and regulates financial institutions, attempts to minimize risk in the financial system, and offers financial services to banks, the government, and foreign financial institutions

Government Agencies

The following are government agencies and their purpose:

- FDA = Food and Drug Administration. Responsible for regulating the safety of foods and dietary supplements, medicinal and pharmaceutical drugs, veterinary products, and cosmetics
- EPA = Environmental Protection Agency. Charged with protecting human health and the environment. Regulates air standards, fuel economy, and water quality
- FEMA = Federal Emergency Management Agency. Coordinates responses to disasters which local and state authorities are unable to address themselves
- FDIC = Federal Deposit Insurance Corporation. Insures deposits at participating financial institutions, currently up to $250,000 per depositor.

US Patent

According to the US Patent Office, the purpose of obtaining a patent is to grant "the right to exclude others from making, using, offering for sale, or selling" the invention created by the patent holder.

- Typically, a patent remains in effect for 20 years from the date when the patent was applied for at the US Patent Office
- The three types of patents are:
- a utility patent, offered to anyone who invents or discovers a new process, machine or device or any "new and useful" modification of an existing such process, etc.
- a design patent, which may be granted to anyone who devises a new and original design for an existing article of manufacture
- a plant patent, to offer patent protection to anyone who invents or discovers and asexually reproduces a new variety of plant
- For further information, go to http://www.uspto.gov

OSHA

The Occupational Safety and Health Act was implemented in 1970 to create the Occupational Safety and Health Administration (OSHA), an agency of the US Department of Labor.

- OSHA's primary stated objective is to ensure that businesses in the private sector provide their workers with safe and healthful working conditions by preventing job-related injuries, illnesses, or fatalities
- OSHA accomplishes these goals through the issuance and the enforcement of its rules, referred to as standards for workplace safety and health
- OSHA initially received considerable criticism for creating what its critics considered confusing and overly burdensome regulations, in addition to what were often characterized as inconsistent and arbitrary enforcement of its rules
- For more information, visit www.osha.gov

INTELLECTUAL PROPERTY

Intellectual property refers to certain types of legal monopolies, specifically the fruits of creations of the mind, such as literary, musical, and other artistic works.

- Intellectual property rights are protected by such legal structures as patents, copyrights, and trademarks
- The main economic principle behind the concept of intellectual property is that in conferring legal protection upon these works, the monopoly profits derived there from offer financial incentives for innovation, research, and development of the properties under its jurisdiction
- Economists estimate that a significant percentage of economic growth can be directly attributed to the concept of intellectual property
- One criticism of the concept of intellectual property is that it indiscriminately lumps together a variety of endeavors which would be better differentiated under specific patent or trademark definitions
- Another is that the concept of intellectual property unfairly benefits large corporate interests, to the detriment of the individual inventor

COPYRIGHT

A copyright offers the copyright holder protection for "original works of authorship" such as literary, dramatic, musical, and artistic creations.

- The works need not be published to be afforded such protection
- A copyright offers the copyright holder the exclusive rights to reproduce the copyrighted work, to distribute or display the copyrighted work, and to create derivative variations of the copyrighted work
- Note that a copyright does not protect the subject matter of the copyrighted work, but only its specific form of expression

TRADEMARK

A trademark is a word, name, symbol, or device which is used to identify a product and to distinguish the trademarked product from other similar products designed by others.

- A trademark prevents others from utilizing a confusingly similar word or symbol but does not prevent others from creating a similar product or service
- For further information, go to http://www.uspto.gov

ENTREPRENEURSHIP

Simply put, entrepreneurship is the act of initiating a new business enterprise.

- The most common interpretation of entrepreneurship is the case of an individual or a group of individuals who start an entirely new business, although it may also refer to that of an individual or a group of individuals who initiate a significant enhancement to an existing business
- The essential tasks in launching an entrepreneurial endeavor are:
    - Coming up with an idea for the new enterprise
    - Developing a business plan for the venture
    - Assembling the capital and human resources required to get the enterprise started
    - Utilizing these resources to create the physical manifestation of the business
    - Promoting the business in such a way as to create public awareness and attract customers

SBA

The Small Business Administration (SBA) is a US government agency whose primary mission is to provide assistance to small businesses and to communities which have been struck by disaster.

- The SBA provides loans directly to business or may serve as the guarantor of loans provided by financial institutions such as banks
- Having directly or indirectly helped something like 20,000 small businesses, the SBA is the single largest backer of businesses in the country
- The core of the SBA's operations consists of the various loan programs it offers
- Contrary to a common misconception, the SBA loan programs are not designed for at-risk borrowers, such as those with bad credit, and they do not provide start-up funding; rather, these programs generally offer longer terms and more lenient affordability requirements than conventional bank loans

SBA TYPES OF LOANS

The SBA loan types are as follows:

- Loan Guarantee Program: Helps small entrepreneurs to start a business or to expand an existing business
- Microloans Program: Provides up to $35,000 to small business which can't get financing from the traditional banking community
- Economic Development Program: Provides free counseling and low-cost training to small businesses
- Business Development Program: Helps socially and economically challenged business owners
- 504 Fixed Asset Financing Program: Provides capital for purchasing land or for construction

OUTSOURCING AND INSOURCING

Outsourcing is the practice whereby a company contracts with another company to perform some or all of those functions that could also be or usually have been provided in-house.

- By contrast, insourcing is the practice whereby a company chooses to perform one or more of these functions in-house, rather than to contract the work out to an external entity
- Outsourcing frequently employs businesses in other countries to perform many of the functions that have usually been regarded as intrinsic to managing a business, occasionally the entire information management of a company
- In the United States, a great number of jobs, especially in the field of information technology (IT), have been outsourced to various foreign firms, commonly in India, where wages are significantly cheaper than in the United States
- The impact on workers in IT has been significant, resulting in the layoffs of large numbers of workers in this field
- Outsourcing can occur when a US company replaces permanent employees with contractors and temporary workers

ENTREPRENEUR OBSTACLES

Entrepreneurship is an inherently difficult undertaking.

- The great majority of new businesses fail, whether from unrealistic expectations of demand for the product, faulty execution in developing the product, or unrealistic financial planning
- Mainly, it is difficult to come up with an idea which is both truly innovative and practically feasible
- It is easy to become enthralled by an idea to the extent that unrealistic visions of its success obscure the obstacles involved, such as the difficulties in obtaining funding or the failure to acknowledge the extent of competition from existing businesses
- An entrepreneurial endeavor may fail because its initiator has grossly underestimated the amount of effort it will require

REVENUE

Revenue is the total amount of money a business receives for the goods and services it provides over a specific time period.

PROFIT

Profit is the positive gain a business obtains after the costs of all operating expenses are subtracted from total revenue.

LOSS

Loss is the opposite of profit. The condition which occurs when total revenue is less than operating expenses.

RISK

Risk is the likelihood of loss or of less than expected profit.

STANDARD OF LIVING

Standard of living is the quantity of goods and services one can purchase with the amount of money one has. Also refers to the financial health of a population.

QUALITY OF LIFE

Quality of life is the general well-being of individuals and of society. Not limited to financial wealth, but also includes environmental, political, and social freedoms and protections.

INFORMATION TECHNOLOGY (IT)

The microchip has been at the heart of the technological advances in the late 20th and 21st centuries. It lies at the heart of modern computer and communications systems and has revolutionized manufacturing through the implementation of robots. Among the devices and services utilizing microchips are computers, copiers, medical imaging devices, telephones, cell phones, and, of course, the Internet. The principal areas of impact of these technological advances have been in:

- Productivity, where ever-greater amounts of work can now be performed in increasingly less time
- Effectiveness, where the desired result can be achieved with a greater degree of accuracy
- Efficiency, in which more goods and services can be produced while expending less effort and resources

GOVERNMENT PROMOTING ENTREPRENEURSHIP

By permitting private ownership of businesses; here in the United States, we often take this concept for granted. But in some countries, the government owns most of the businesses, limiting the viability of entrepreneurship.

- By passing laws that allow businesses to write contracts with legal weight. By so doing, government reduces the risk of embarking on an entrepreneurial enterprise
- By establishing a universally recognized currency. This enables a business to purchase and sell goods and services using that currency
- By defining and enforcing remedies to corruption. Corruption in many countries makes it extremely difficult to do business there or to conduct business relationships with their companies

RECENT DEMOGRAPHIC TRENDS

One demographic development has been the emergence of a diverse population.

- This newly constituted customer base has led many companies to hire a more representatively diverse workforce to serve their interests
- Over 75 percent of Fortune 1000 companies have implemented some kind of diversity program
- Another development has been the aging of the US population
- Experts calculate that by the year 2020 over 23 percent of the population will be over 60 years of age
- These older Americans are now the richest demographic in the country and have significant buying power, leading businesses to design products and services for their needs
- Finally, the dramatic growth of two-income families and single parents has led to companies offering such programs as parental and family leave, flexible work hours, and counseling

Companies Surviving and Thriving

The most important way to maintain a competitive edge is by producing a superior product. A product with significant known defects is at a disadvantage out of the gate.

- However, merely producing a superior product will not automatically guarantee success if it is not accompanied by outstanding service and excellent value
- The adage "The customer is always right" cannot be overemphasized, and the success of such customer-oriented companies as Nordstrom department stores and Disney exemplify this philosophy
- One way in which business can successfully implement this principle is to develop an empowered workforce, in which frontline workers are given the training, responsibility, freedom, and the opportunity to respond to customer needs and to make decisions which will advance the company's business objectives

Farming Industry Technological Innovations

Technological developments such as the cotton gin and improvements to farm machinery have greatly increased the efficiency and productivity of farming.

- And the rise of giant corporate farms has contributed to the diminution in the number and size of family farms, to the extent that the number of family farms has decreased from roughly 5.7 million at the turn of the 20th century to fewer than 2 million today. This change has predictably resulted in the elimination of many jobs
- The manufacturing industry, like the farming industry, has also experienced job attrition as a result of technological advancement. Many of the workers who were displaced from the manufacturing sector have found work in service industries, where the emphasis on the production of goods has been replaced by the delivery of intangible products such as education, insurance, and tourism
- Now, services constitute over half of the American economy and have produced almost all of its increases in employment

Iraq and Afghanistan Affect on the American Economy

The wars in Iraq and Afghanistan have consumed hundreds of billions of American dollars, which have been deemed necessary to provide the materiel and manpower to prosecute these conflicts.

- That these dollars might have been spent elsewhere—for example, on infrastructure, education, or creation of more readily accessible health care for all Americans—has been a source of controversy and the subject of much debate
- Further, following the terrorist attacks on September 11, 2001, many companies have had to focus increasing efforts and commit substantial financial resources to reduce their vulnerability to terrorist attack, adding significantly to their operating costs
- Airlines, for example, have had to build stronger cockpits, purchase more detection equipment, and hire new security personnel

Proliferation of Personal Electronic Data

Companies routinely store vast amounts of information about their customers in computer files called databases.

- These files contain such information as customer names, addresses, telephone numbers, credit information, and buying histories
- This data enables companies to identify individual purchasing patterns, which they can employ to target marketing efforts such as catalogs, direct mail, and e-mail campaigns
- Companies frequently trade and share their databases with other companies, enabling many retailers to have access to great volumes of data which they individually would be unable to assemble
- This sharing of data gives rise to the possibility of such data being leaked to less than reputable entities, which can use the data to commit such criminal acts as fraud and identity theft, a crime which the FTC estimates to affect some 10 million Americans annually

E-Commerce Alters Business Landscape

E-commerce refers to the buying and selling of goods and services over the Internet, a phenomenon which burst onto the scene in the early 1990s and which no business today can afford to ignore.

- Traditional businesses must learn how to react to the new forms of competition advanced by their competitors through their use of the Internet
- A great number of companies arose virtually overnight in an attempt to exploit this new business venue, and many of them have failed or have seen their stock prices sink dramatically due to their failure to accurately judge the marketplace or to efficiently adapt their business practices to this new endeavor

There are two main types of E-commerce:

- Business-to-consumer (B2C), in which businesses attempt to sell their products or services directly to consumers
- Business-to-business (B2B), where goods or services are sold from one business to another

Micropreneurship

Micropreneurs have found a way to start their own small businesses without having to commit to the idea of growing them into large corporate entities.

- The great advantage for these individuals is that they get to work at home, rather than commuting to a high-pressure corporate job
- Home-based businesses have access to the same type of computer technology as their large corporate competitors, making it relatively inexpensive to start up
- Tax laws also favor such individuals, since there are now significant deductions for home offices

Among the challenges faced by micropreneurs are:

- The difficulty of attracting customers in the absence of an external place of business
- Effective time management takes self-discipline, often in the face of less than stellar monetary recompense
- It can be difficult to balance work and the family tasks that occur in the home
- Micropreneurs may have to bear the cost of additions to their insurance policies

NONPROFIT ORGANIZATION

A nonprofit company is one in which the owners or organizers are not motivated primarily by a quest for personal financial gain.

- Nonprofit organizations are often devoted to social causes, such as public schools, charities, or environmental protection serving the general good
- As such, nonprofits often attract individuals who strive to provide some social, environmental, or educational benefit to society
- Despite nonprofit companies' emphasis on providing what they perceive as needed public services as opposed to financial gain, for them to be successful they must employ sound business practices to survive and promote their interests
- Since not all entrepreneurs are good managers, an entrepreneur who endeavors to form a nonprofit organization must ensure that a competent management structure is in place to properly employ leadership, information management, marketing and financial expertise to the enterprise

ENTREPRENEUR FUND SOURCES

The Small Business Administration (SBA), while its primary mission is not lending money, does have a microloan program which provides loans of up to $35,000 to small business owners.

- The Small Business Investment Company (SBIC) is composed of individual companies which are licensed by the SBA to provide loans to small businesses
- Small Business Development Centers (SBDCs) are private financial institutions which are authorized by the SBA to loan money to small businesses. In addition to lending money, SBDCs can offer valuable assistance in evaluating business ideas and developing business plans
- Venture capital of individual investors, otherwise known as angel investors, is a primary source of funding for many entrepreneurs. Venture capitalists, however, often ask for a significant percentage of the entrepreneur's profits, which can result in the entrepreneur losing control of his business

WEB-BASED BUSINESSES

The principal advantage of operating a Web-based business is that the business owner is his own boss, as opposed to working for someone else.

- In an era of increasing unemployment, this type of business may be especially attractive to an unemployed person
- Web-based businesses are typically quite inexpensive to start—all that is initially required is a home computer and access to a Web-hosting service

The main challenge faced by an individual seeking to start a Web-based business is the great proliferation of others seeking to do exactly the same thing.

- A rule of thumb is that if you can think it up, somebody else may very well have also come up with the same or a similar idea
- Finally, it is easy to underestimate the commitments of time and energy which will be required to create a viable Web-based business

Business Plan Components

A typical business plan is between 25 and 50 pages and contains the following sections:

- *Company description*: A high-level overview of how the different elements of the company fit together
- *Executive summary*: The most important section of the business plan. Consists of a concise overview of the company and its objectives
- *Market analysis*: Identifies the primary industry of the company, as well as identifying the target market
- *Financial plan*: In addition to historical financial data, describes forecasted income and expenses
- *Marketing plan*: Identifies market penetration strategy, channels of distribution, and sales strategy.
- *Capital required*: The amount of funds required to initiate the business and to continue operations
- *Manufacturing plan*: Describes the resources required to produce the company's product

Overseas Markets and Small Business

The primary attraction to going international is that there are billions of potential customers worldwide, while there are only a few hundred million such potential customers in the United States. Additionally, small businesses are not burdened by the bureaucratic inefficiencies of huge corporations, enabling them to make quick decisions and to deliver their products more easily.

- The main hurdle a small business encounters in going international is the difficulty in obtaining financing
- Few domestic businesses have sufficient capital to embark on such a venture on their own
- Another hurdle may be encountered when attempting to operate in a foreign culture, without knowing how to adapt to these cultural differences. And there is often a daunting amount of bureaucracy involved in going global

Population Growth or Population Decline Impact

In countries in the developing world such as those in North Africa and West Asia, rapid population growth may be contributing to greater poverty and its resultant civil unrest.

- Some economists believe that population growth can lead to a more vibrant economy and better economic conditions for a country's citizens, especially if the populace is well educated
- Population decline, on the other hand, is not necessarily a remedy for the poverty which can result from outsized population growth
- In some industrial countries, specifically Japan, Italy, and Russia, declines in population can lead to a situation where there are a greater number of older citizens and fewer young ones to care for them
- In the United States, for example, the contributions of younger citizens to the Social Security system may not be sufficient to provide retirement income to the "baby boom" generation which is now entering retirement

ECONOMICS

Economics is a social science concerned with how a society utilizes resources in the production, distribution, and consumption of goods and services. Also, the study of theory and management of economies or economic systems

MACROECONOMICS

Macroeconomics is the study of a nation's economy as a whole, in terms of its total income and output and the interrelationship among diverse economic sectors

MICROECONOMICS

Microeconomics is the study of individual components of a nation's economy, such as employment within specific industries and patterns of supply and demand in individual markets

RESOURCE DEVELOPMENT

Resource development is the study of how to develop and increase resources and methods of utilizing such resources in the most efficient and productive manner

RESUME REFERENCES

In the case of references for a resume, be very selective.

- References should provide strong, candid statements about the applicant's professionalism and quality as an employee or coworker
- Once a person agrees to be a reference for you, they may need to write a letter of recommendation, be available to speak to the prospective employer via phone or email, or may need to complete reference forms
- In any case, do not ask someone to serve as a reference if you are unsure about their feelings about you

CAPITALISM

Capitalism is an economic system in which a significant portion of the means of production and distribution of a nation's goods and services is privately or corporately owned, as opposed to being owned by the government.

- Capitalism is the foundation of the economy of the United States, as well as the economies of England, Canada, and most other developed nations
- In a capitalistic system, individuals and companies have the right to own and use wealth, whether in the form of capital, production facilities, or/and distribution systems, to employ labor and to earn income with little or no government control
- Note, however, that no country is purely capitalist, as government is often involved in such issues as setting minimum wages, establishing standards for working conditions, and enforcing environmental and safety regulations

Free Markets

Free markets are defined as business operating under the principles of supply and demand, without the intervention or regulation of government, except to protect against fraud or other illegal practices.

- Free markets exist in contrast to controlled, or regulated, markets, in which government directly or indirectly sets prices and supplies
- Under free markets, demand from consumers is the engine that drives the production and sale of goods and services
- In free markets it is the marketplace itself that determines the price of these goods and services; that is, sellers strive to produce a product that is desired in the marketplace, and then seek to arrive at a price which buyers will find acceptable

Capitalism's Four Fundamental Rights

The right to private property. This right is the cornerstone of capitalism. It refers to the individual's right to own, purchase, sell, rent, utilize, transfer, and exchange land, buildings, equipment, and other such similar tangible assets.

The right to own a business and to profit from its operation. A business's profits are the property of the business owner, minus the taxes taken out by the government.

The right to be free to compete. Individuals are permitted, within certain limits established by government, to compete with other individuals or businesses to produce and offer for sale goods or services in the public marketplace.

The right to freedom of choice. Individuals are free to choose where they want to reside, what occupation they wish to enter, and what products or services they wish to produce and sell.

Free Market Inequities

Free markets have the potential to enrich managers and business owners while lower-level employees earn substantially less.

- Workers with more limited means or who are in ill health may have a hard time competing in such a free-wheeling environment
- An extreme example of these types of inequities can be found in the use of such practices as child labor and slavery
- Another very real danger in free markets is that greed may drive some business people to various forms of unethical conduct
- The recent economic crisis is considered by many to exemplify these dangers, as top managers and CEOs manipulated the system to enrich themselves by promoting such high-risk practices as derivatives and credit-default swaps

Competition in Free Markets

Perfect competition: The market situation in which the marketplace consists of many sellers producing a homogeneous product, thus preventing any individual seller from unilaterally dictating the price of the product

Monopolistic competition: The market situation in which many sellers produce products which are similar but which buyers perceive as distinct. Here, product differentiation is paramount to a seller's success

Oligopoly: The market condition in which there are very few sellers, thus conferring upon any one seller the ability to substantially affect prices among all such sellers

Monopoly: Describes that market condition in which a single seller is the only one producing a particular product or service and thus has absolute control over the price of that product or service

Free-Market Economies and Command Economies

Free-market economies, commonly referred to as capitalist, are defined as those in which goods and services are produced and distributed in response to demand in the marketplace.

- By contrast, under the command economies found in socialist and communist systems, it is the government that to a large extent determines what products and services will be produced
- The limitations of each of these economies have resulted in a trend in which each type increasingly adopts principles of the other, resulting in what is referred to as mixed economies
- Previously communist nations such as Russia now permit some degree of private ownership; and some capitalist nations such as England and France now permit increased government regulation
- In fact, in response to the current economic crisis, the United States is moving to adopt increased regulation of financial markets, to the dismay of some advocates of free-market capitalism

Socialism

Socialism is an economic system espousing collective or government ownership of some or most of a nation's core businesses.

- Under socialism, the profits generated by these businesses are more equally distributed among the populace, thus reducing economic inequality
- A greater degree of social equality is achieved through the redistribution of wealth from more affluent members of society to those of lesser means
- Proponents of socialism point to the tendency of capitalist societies to have great disparities in wealth between the well-off and the working class
- Another benefit advanced by proponents of socialism is that of universal free education and health care
- The most commonly identified negative consequence of socialism is that, in redistributing wealth, it stifles innovation and entrepreneurship

Productivity

Productivity is the measure of the quantity of goods and services which can be produced in a given span of time.

- Increases in productivity result in higher gross earnings (assuming markets exist for the product or service in question) and consequently higher profits, as a given worker is capable of producing a greater quantity within a given time period
- Because a large portion of the US economy is in the service sector, increased productivity in this area presents particular challenges, specifically because technological innovations tend not to be capable of increasing productivity for such workers as teachers, attorneys, and others

- Technological innovations, especially computers and other data processing systems, have greatly increased productivity in many areas of the economy, such as manufacturing (where robots now perform jobs previously accomplished by many workers) and any enterprise in which large quantities of data are a central component

Economic Conditions

Three main indicators of economic conditions are the following:

- *Gross domestic product (GDP)*: The total value of all goods and services produced in a nation in any given year. GDP represents the sum of all consumer investment, and government spending, plus the value of exports, minus the value of imports.
- *The unemployment rate*: This is a measure of the percentage of a nation's total workforce that is currently out of work, is seeking work, and has tried to find a job within the previous four weeks. As of November 2009, the unemployment rate in the United States hit a 26-year high of 10.2 percent. But this number does not include those workers who have given up seeking work or who are underemployed, as in working part-time jobs.

The Price Indexes:

- The rate of inflation or deflation is that at which the general prices of goods are increasing or decreasing
- The Consumer Price Index (CPI), also called the cost-of-living index, measures fluctuations in the price of such services as housing, electricity, and food
- The Producer Price Index (PPI) measures prices at the wholesale level

Fiscal Policy

Fiscal policy is how governments attempt to stabilize the economy by increasing or decreasing revenue collection (taxes) and by increasing or decreasing spending.

- In theory, high taxes result in a less robust economy, as they discourage businesses from expanding by limiting the amount of profit a company makes, thus making the enterprise less attractive
- As a corollary, lower taxes supposedly create economic growth, as the lure of higher profits attracts new business ventures to be created and existing businesses to expand
- On the spending side, governments spend their accumulated revenue on a variety of things, such as highways, the armed forces, police, education, and health care
- The national deficit is the amount of money the government spends, typically annually, over the amount it accumulates through revenue collection
- The national debt is the sum total of government deficits over time

Business Cycle Phrases

Economic boom: An easy to understand concept, which means that business is doing exceptionally well

Recession: Technically, two or more consecutive quarters in which there is a decline in GDP (gross domestic product). In a recession, consumers purchase fewer and less expensive products, unemployment goes up, and there is a tangible drop in the standard of living

Depression: A severe recession, often defined as one in which the GDP declines more than 10 percent. While there have been a number of recessions in recent history, the only true depression occurred in the Great Depression of 1929–1933

Recovery: The phenomenon which occurs in the business cycle when a recession or depression turns around and the economy begins to grow again. Note that recovery does not necessarily imply higher employment, as appears to be the case in the current economy, which is said to be recovering but where job losses continue to mount

MONEY

Money is anything purchasers can use to obtain goods and services from sellers. Until the advent of modern currencies, many diverse objects served as money, from shells to feathers, stones, and livestock. The use of money contrasts with barter, in which goods and services are directly traded for other goods and services. Among the advantages conferred by the use of money are:

- *Portability*: it is much easier to carry around than bulky material goods
- *Divisibility*: varying sizes of currency and coins can be used to represent different values
- *Stability*: large populations, often across national borders, can come to agree on the value of a specific type of money (due to its stability, the US dollar has become the most commonly agreed upon international measure of value)
- *Durability*: coins (as contrasted with paper currency) can endure for thousands of years
- *Uniqueness:* at least until the advent of modern copiers and printers, it has been difficult to counterfeit currency

MONETARY POLICY AND FISCAL POLICY

In contrast to fiscal policy, which concerns itself with taxes and spending, monetary policy refers to the activities of a central bank (in the United States, the Federal Reserve, or "the Fed") to influence the economy by managing the money supply and by setting interest rates.

- With regard to managing the money supply, the Fed may decrease the amount of money in the system in order to slow what is perceived as overheated growth in the economy; or the Fed may increase the amount of money in order to stimulate economic growth in what is perceived as a sluggish economy
- With regard to setting interest rates, the Fed tends to raise interest rates when the economy is booming, thus making it more expensive for businesses to borrow money; by contrast, the Fed is inclined to lower interest rates when the economy is sluggish by making it easier for businesses to borrow. In these ways, the Fed can theoretically mitigate against wild fluctuations in the economy

COMMERCIAL BANKS

Commercial banks are institutions designed to make a profit for their owners and stockholders. These institutions service two types of customers: depositors and borrowers. Commercial banks receive deposits from individuals and corporations and hold these deposits in checking and savings accounts; they then use these funds to make loans to borrowers.

SAVINGS AND LOANS

Like commercial banks, savings and loans—also known as thrift institutions—receive deposits into checking and savings accounts and use these funds to finance home mortgage loans for their customers.

CREDIT UNIONS

Credit unions are nonprofit financial institutions which are owned by their members and offer a full variety of banking services. As a result of their nonprofit status, credit unions pay no federal income tax. Thus they are able to offer loans with relatively lower interest rates and interest on deposits at higher rates than commercial banks or savings and loans

Weak or Falling Dollar

When the value of the US dollar falls, holders of dollars are able to purchase fewer goods and services for their dollars.

- The dollar generally becomes weaker as a response to the perceived strength of the US economy
- The consequences of a weak dollar in terms of international commerce is that US goods become relatively cheaper in foreign countries, thus benefiting the export of US goods, while foreign goods become more expensive for US buyers, thus making foreign exporters realize greater profits

Strong or Rising Dollar

By contrast, when the dollar rises, it becomes stronger relative to foreign currencies.

- As a result, US exports suffer from being more expensive in foreign countries, and foreign imports into the United States become cheaper for American buyers

World Bank

The World Bank while not a bank in the traditional sense is designed to finance economic development through providing low-interest loans, interest-free credits, and grants to developing countries, in order to increase productivity and raise their standard of living.

- The services of the World Bank are designed to provide financial assistance to developing countries in the fields of education, health, and natural resource management

IMF

The International Monetary Fund (IMF) consists of 184 individual member-countries. Its mission is to encourage cooperative international monetary policies and promote exchange rate stability.

- The basic principle guiding the IMF's activities is to provide stability to the international monetary system
- The IMF, unlike the World Bank, is not primarily a lending institution, though in recent years it has provided billions of dollars to countries whose currencies had dropped precipitously
- Recently, a significant number of these loans have failed to achieve their intended goals, and as a result the IMF has come under heated criticism

Internet Banking

The rapid rise in the use of the Internet has affected banking in significant ways, principally in that financial institutions now permit their customers online access to their accounts.

- This enables depositors to handle many of their financial transactions from their homes
- Depositors can now use their phones or their computers to check the balances of their accounts, transfer funds from one account to another, apply for credit or loans, and pay mortgage/rent bills, utility bills, etc
- In fact, there are now banks that are exclusively present on the Internet, having no "brick and mortar" facilities whatsoever

- But many depositors desire the personal interaction they can obtain at only traditional brick-and-mortar banks.
- Those financial institutions which offer both online and personal access appear to be the most viable in the foreseeable future

MANAGEMENT EVOLVEMENT

In the past, managers were referred to as "bosses" and occupied higher strata within a business organization than the workers within their purview.

- Managers in the past were frequently tasked with getting the most out of their workers through a system of rewards and punishment, such as praise or expressions of disapproval
- More recently managers have migrated into a much less parental role, in which teamwork and cooperation are emphasized over discipline and the dispensing of orders
- This new approach is, at least in part, a response to the reality that in today's highly technical environment many of those workers a manager supervises are now more technically proficient than the managers themselves
- Managers out of necessity must place more trust in their employees' decisions and actions, resulting in a more egalitarian work environment

MANAGEMENT

Management is that process, employed in both human endeavors and in all business activity, which seeks to get people together to accomplish specific goals and objectives.

- Managers define the objectives of a business enterprise and design a framework in which members of the enterprise can work together to provide the enterprise with the focus and motivation to accomplish the business efforts of the organization
- Among the primary functions of management is to analyze available organizational resources (such as employees), financial resources, and physical resources (such as plants and equipment) and to maximize the effectiveness of these resources

ORGANIZING

Organizing is the essential management process by which a business designs the structure of the organization, both in terms of the physical structures and equipment needed to produce the company's products and in terms of the human resources required to carry out the functions of the enterprise.

- The objective is to set up an environment in which all the various pieces of the business function together to most efficiently produce, market, and distribute the company's product
- Organizational objectives are necessarily focused around meeting customer needs and designing processes to most efficiently deliver products that meet these needs
- Inevitably, circumstances in the marketplace change and management must maintain the willingness and the flexibility to review its organizational structure to adapt to these new conditions

Planning

Planning is the process by which management anticipates trends and devises the most ideal strategies which a business needs to adopt to meet these challenges.

- Planning inevitably involves setting goals in order to meet what are perceived to be future developments in the marketplace
- Perhaps the most fundamental objective addressed by planning is to determine how best to satisfy the business's customer needs
- This objective may be fulfilled by creating new products or modifying or updating the products a business sells; or by determining and implementing strategies to provide more efficient and congenial services to customers
- These days a company often employs a planning team to accomplish these ends

Management Practices

A business must have clearly defined standards and procedures in order to function efficiently.

- It must also have concrete ways to monitor performance and measure results, and to analyze these results in terms of their contribution to the organization's business objectives
- A business must also provide workers with a system of rewards and a venue for constructive criticism, in order that these workers have a frame of reference to determine in what ways they are making positive contributions to the enterprise and in what ways they can modify their approach to more effectively perform their obligations

Leadership

Leadership may be defined as the process of social influence, whereby one person or a group of people organize and motivate others to best accomplish the goals of an organization.

- Effective leaders design and create the framework to accomplish an organization's objectives and assemble the personnel and physical resources to best achieve those objectives
- Effective leadership combines the capacity of leaders to listen and observe with the ability to articulate its values and visions, and to create an environment in which the employees of an organization can accomplish its goals and are motivated to do so
- Effective leadership also involves being able and willing to identify problems and having the flexibility to adapt to changing circumstances

Mission Statement

The purpose of a mission statement is to create in concrete terms an organization's fundamental purposes. A mission statement should address the following concerns:

- *The organization's self-concept*: How does the organization perceive its identity and role in the marketplace?
- *The organization's philosophy*: What values will the organization apply to its operations to best fulfill its mission?
- *Long-term survival*: How does the organization perceive the future, and will the organization prepare for future developments?
- *Customer needs*: What are customers' needs and the concrete strategies to fulfill them?

- *Social responsibility*: How will the company advance its values in the service of the community?
- *The company's product or service*: What specifically will the company produce, distribute, and sell to meet its business and social responsibilities?

Business Vision

Management's first task in planning an organization's structure is to define the vision for the organization.

- A vision is much broader than simply a goal; a vision is an encompassing description of the organization's purpose and its future
- Among the goals of devising an organization's vision are to impart a sense of purpose to the organization's goals, ideally in such a manner as to inspire workers to unite in a common pursuit to attain those goals
- Without a clear vision, a business lacks focus and direction, with different sectors within the business working at cross-purposes
- As a result, the business will be in a strategically weaker position than its competitors and will have difficulty correcting its course of action to respond to the imperatives of the marketplace

Strategy

Strategy is a plan by which an organization seeks to accomplish its major objectives. Strategic planning involves devising the policies, procedures, and methods which an organization will employ in order to achieve its long-term goals. Some of the considerations that go into strategic planning are:

- Deciding what products or services the company intends to produce and sell
- Deciding who its customer base will be
- Determining in what geographic areas the company intends to compete
- Identifying the human and physical resources which will be needed for the company to accomplish its business aims
- In today's fast-changing world, strategic planning needs to be flexible and adaptable, attributes without which a company's strategic planning may limit its ability to respond to changing conditions

Goals and Objectives

Goals may be described as the long-term objectives an organization seeks to achieve.

- Goals are used to motivate and inspire employees and to give them a concrete target to strive to attain
- Goals are not merely handed down from management to employees, which could result in employees feeling dictated to and left out of the decision-making process. Rather, goals are set and agreed upon in a collaborative context

Objectives, by contrast, are short-term steps in the service of achieving the organization's goals.

- By breaking down goals into more bite-sized objectives, workers avoid feeling overwhelmed by a process in which the rewards remain far in the future
- Objectives give workers the satisfaction of regularly achieving small successes, thus motivating them to continue to work in the service of the longer-term goals of the organization

Functions of Business

Organizational Planning

Organizational planning refers to the process of setting standards and schedules in order to achieve a business's objectives.

- Organizational planning may be considered a tool for managers to measure how successfully an organization is accomplishing its stated goals
- In contrast to strategic planning, which concerns itself with a company's overall direction, organizational planning concerns itself with the daily operations of specific departments, as well as the managers and employees within those departments
- Organizational planning deals with an organization's immediate objectives and with formulating strategies to achieve these objectives
- Additionally, organizational planning also entails such specifics as establishing proper staffing and defining the resources necessary to accomplish the task at hand
- An organizational plan may also include timelines which detail when certain tasks are to be completed

Tactics

In contrast to strategic planning, tactical planning refers to defining and developing short-term objectives to be achieved in the service of accomplishing the goals identified in strategic planning.

- Tactical planning typically involves decision making performed by managers and workers at lower levels of an organization than those personnel making strategic decisions
- Tactical planning often concerns itself with identifying the resources and methods by which a specific objective is to be reached
- Whereas blunders in strategic planning can have catastrophic consequences, tactical errors can be more easily remedied and thus prove less damaging

Problem Solving vs. Decision Making

Decision making is often a laborious process, requiring extended analysis of a situation and its possible resolution.

- Problem solving, on the other hand, refers to devising immediate solutions to arising situations, occasionally in the absence of complete information
- Problem solving is an activity that takes place continually throughout the day as obstacles requiring quick resolution are encountered
- Also in contrast to decision making, there is no formal strategy involved in problem solving, which often involves identifying a problem and applying one's experience and ingenuity to devise a solution
- A common approach to problem solving is brainstorming, in which two or more workers devise a variety of possible solutions in a short time span
- Another approach is called PMI, short for listing the pluses, minuses, and implications of potential solutions

Decision Making

In essence, decision making may be defined as the process in which management chooses between two or more alternatives to accomplish a given task. The seven D's of decision making are:

- The situation and assemble what information is needed
- Develop alternative solutions to a problem
- Develop agreement among those addressing the situation
- Decide which alternative will best accomplish the desired goal
- Do the tasks required
- Determine whether the chosen alternative was effective, and follow up if necessary
- The distinction between technical skills, human relations skills, and conceptual skills

Management Skills

Three different skills are necessary in different proportions for top managers, middle managers, and first-line managers and they are the following:

- Technical skills are those that allow a worker to accomplish tasks in a specific discipline, such as computer programming or running a lathe, or within a specific department, such as accounting. Typically, these skills are less important the higher up the organizational ladder the worker is
- Human relations skills come into play when managers deal with such issues as communication and motivation. Some of the characteristics associated with human relations skills are leadership, delegation, offering of support, and morale building. Human relations skills become more important as one moves up the corporate hierarchy
- Conceptual skills involve viewing the organization as a whole and understanding how its various components are supposed to interact and cooperate in the service of advancing the company's goals. Top managers are those employees for whom conceptual skills are the most important, as these skills include planning, organizing, decision making, and problem analysis

Firm's Organizational Levels

The typical organizational levels in a firm are three managerial plus one other:

- The highest level is for top management. Top management encompasses the president of the company, the chief executive officer (CEO) often the president of the company), the chief operation officer (COO), the chief financial officer (CFO), and the chief information officer (CIO)
- The second-highest level is for middle management. This level is composed of general managers, division managers, branch managers, and plant managers
- The next level comprises supervisory management personnel. These employees are often referred to as first-line managers and are those individuals who are directly responsible for supervising workers. Their tasks also include evaluating workers' daily performance
- The next level consists of nonsupervisory employees, workers who are computer programmers, machinists, line cooks, secretaries, etc.

STAFFING IMPORTANCE

Staffing is crucial to the success of an enterprise, as it involves recruiting, selecting, hiring, motivating, and retaining the best possible personnel to advance the company's strategic goals.

- Recruiting and selecting high-quality employees are a fundamental requirement if a company wants to best exploit its market position
- In the past, many employees expected to spend their entire working careers with a single company
- But employee mobility has become much more prevalent of late, with many workers often changing jobs every few years
- This is especially true in IT (information technology) where rapid technological changes naturally result in significant employee turnover
- Once a valued employee is hired, it is in the company's best interest to try to retain him, which is usually accomplished by offering him competitive salary and benefits and by providing a congenial work environment

COMPANY STAKEHOLDERS

A company's stakeholders are any persons or group of persons who are affected by the company's policies and products.

- Stakeholders may be customers, employees, suppliers, and persons living in the company's community
- Recently, companies have been changing their organizational structures and modifying their missions to become more responsive to the needs and desires of customers. As a result, some larger firms have restructured into smaller, more targeted units which it is believed can focus more effectively on customer needs
- Technological advances have been instrumental in providing the impetus for this new orientation, as the Internet makes it much easier for dialogue to occur between companies and customers
- The Internet also makes it easier for companies to interact with suppliers, distributors, and retailers
- Firms are forming partnerships and engaging in joint ventures, often on an international level, making effective communication essential to maintaining cohesive business strategies

AUTOCRATIC LEADERSHIP

Autocratic leadership is that in which a leader or manager makes decisions on her own, without input from peers.

- Autocratic leadership isn't necessarily a bad thing; in fact, it may be the most effective type of leadership in an emergency or a crisis
- Autocratic leadership may also be effective in situations where new, inexperienced, or unskilled workers will benefit under the direction of an uncompromising and energetic leader who will convey to them exactly what their responsibilities are and how to carry them out
- When autocratic leadership is employed indiscriminately or in inappropriate circumstances, it likely will prove to be counterproductive, in that the autocratic leader will be resented, and her perceived insensitivity to the needs of others may lead to resistance or rebellion from the employees under her leadership

Management and Leadership

The main objective of management is to attempt to provide order and stability within an organization. By contrast, leadership provides a vision for the enterprise to pursue, including such endeavors as setting corporate values and ethics and attempting to mold the organization to maximize its effectiveness. The four principal characteristics of leadership are:

- Developing a corporate vision. Motivate others in the organization to want to help achieve that vision
- Defining corporate values. Identify how the company will best serve the needs of customers, employees, communities, and the environment
- Delineating and promoting corporate ethics. This includes the honest and fair treatment of employees of the company, as well as its customers and business associates
- Embracing change. A leader must be able to identify and react to an ever-changing marketplace and must adapt to new circumstances to further the company's goals

Empowering Workers

The concept of empowering workers is a relatively new one, and it contrasts with the practices of the recent past, in which managers assumed the more autocratic role of giving assignments and instructions and setting rules, a practice known as directing.

- The concept of empowering workers is to involve employees in the decision-making process
- One of the principal motivating factors behind adopting a business environment in which workers are empowered is that in such an environment, workers presumably will feel like more active participants in the organization and thus will put forth greater effort and willingly accept more responsibility
- Some managers, however, are reluctant to relinquish their power to make decisions more or less unilaterally and to have the sole ability to enforce adherence to their rules

Participative Leadership vs. Autocratic Leadership

Participative leadership, otherwise referred to as democratic leadership, occurs when managers work together with employees in making decisions and formulating strategies and tactics to accomplish the business objectives of the organization.

- By contrast, under autocratic leadership, decisions are arrived at and strategies are devised by the leader personally, in the absence of consultation with employees
- Participative leadership doesn't necessarily lead to an organization's increased effectiveness in conducting its business, but it can't be denied that participative leadership results in greater job satisfaction for workers, who feel valued and respected and thus are motivated to contribute to the organization's efforts
- Some of the traits that characterize participative leadership include the ability on the part of management to listen, to accept constructive criticism, and to inspire loyalty on the part of workers

Control Process

The control process specifies how an organization will measure workers' performance as it relates to the accomplishment of specified business objectives, rewarding employees for excellence and taking corrective action when it is required. The five steps of the control process are:

- *Establish standards.* In the absence of clear standards, performance is impossible to measure
- *Monitor performance.* Employ concrete means of measuring performance. Performance against plans. Evaluate whether performance accomplishes the stated objectives
- *Communicate results.* Inform workers as to whether their performance is adequate or not
- *Reward success and take corrective action when necessary.* Provide positive feedback for excellent performance. When performance is substandard, seek ways to improve it

Knowledge Management

Knowledge management refers to the process of gathering the information relevant to an organization's business, finding a place and a manner to store this information, and making it available to those workers for whom it will enhance their ability to do their job. The steps required to implement a system of knowledge management include:

- Determining what information is important and relevant for the functioning of the organization
- Establishing how this information is going to be organized and stored
- Establishing who has access to what portions of this information and how they will be permitted to access it.

One of the benefits of a system of knowledge management is that maintaining information in a central location reduces the chance of duplication of effort. Another benefit is documentation of both successful and unsuccessful efforts, in order to be able to repeat successes and avoid the repetition of failures.

Marketing

The common understanding of marketing revolves around the idea of advertising goods for sale.

- But marketing is a much broader concept, consisting of the activities, the group of institutions, and the processes for creating, communicating, delivering, and exchanging goods and services with customers and clients
- Among the processes implemented in marketing are the conception, planning, pricing, promotion, and distribution of goods and services which are designed to satisfy customer and organizational needs.

Facets of Customer Satisfaction

Ultimately, businesses rise or fall on their ability or inability to achieve customer satisfaction.

- One type of customer satisfaction applies to what are termed external customers
- External customers include dealers, suppliers, and end users of the organization's goods or services
- Another type of customer satisfaction applies to what are termed internal customers

- Internal customers include individuals and divisions within the organization itself who are recipients of services from other individuals and divisions within the organization. For example, the sales force of a company is the internal customer of the company's marketing department, which provides the sales personnel with research

Marketing Strategy Developing

A marketing strategy is composed of all the activities an organization uses in order to promote awareness of its product and to inspire potential customers to want to purchase it.

- There are a multitude of varying activities in developing a marketing strategy, including advertising, public relations, generating publicity for the product(s), spreading word of mouth recommendations, and implementing various promotional sales efforts, such as offering discounts, coupons, rebates, and samples
- The final step in developing a marketing strategy is to provide follow-up services, whereby customers can register their opinion of the product and give feedback as to how effectively the organization has supported the product
- Developing a marketing strategy is an ongoing enterprise, requiring the seller to constantly evaluate his approach and make needed corrections

Four P's of Marketing

Product: Once consumer needs have been researched, an organization begins its process by designing products to meet those needs. A product can be anything from a tangible object to a service that is in demand in the marketplace.

Price: Once an organization has decided upon a product to sell, it is essential that the product be priced in a way that will attract customers and still provide enough revenue to make the organization a profit.

Place: This can refer to the physical location of a place of business, such as a store or restaurant. Or it can refer to the geographical area targeted for the distribution and sale of the company's product.

Promotion: This consists of the various strategies sellers use to inform potential customers of their product and to motivate these customers to want to purchase it.

Components of the Marketing Environment

Global factors: Because of the explosion in the use of the Internet, businesses now have access to consumers in vastly diverse geographical locations.

Technological factors: Again, the technological advances accompanying the Internet enable organizations to acquire vast quantities of information and to store it for fast retrieval.

Sociocultural factors: Marketers must closely pay attention to social trends and changing demographics, which can have a profound impact on marketing strategies.

Competitive factors: It is crucial for marketers to be aware of an organization's competitors in the marketplace. Companies now must be able to adjust their pricing and distribution strategies to take competition into account.

Economic factors: Marketers must be attentive to changes in the economic environment in order to be effective. The current economic downturn, for example, has had a profound impact on organizations' marketing strategies.

MARKETING RESEARCH PROCESS

Defining the business opportunity involves carefully analyzing the present situation in the marketplace and seeking out a variety of potential solutions to best take advantage of the specific conditions in real time. Also, this step takes into consideration the necessity of identifying the information required to make intelligent decisions

Collecting data is accurate and up-to-date information is crucial to a successful venture. Obtaining this information can be accomplished by studying existing data which have been published or are available online. Other strategies include focus groups, questionnaires, surveys, and interviews

Analyzing research data: Once data have been collected, this step involves organizing them into coherent categories and honestly interpreting their implications.

Choosing and implementing a solution. After having conducted the three previous steps, a solution from among the discussed alternatives is selected and put into action.

CONCEPT TESTING

Concept testing involves creating an accurate description of the product or service an organization is attempting to sell and then using quantitative and qualitative methods to evaluate customer responses to that product or service.

- Concept testing can take the form of concept evaluation, in which verbal descriptions or visual images of the product are presented to consumers, after which their likelihood to purchase or try the product is recorded
- Or concept testing can be done in a comparative manner, in which the organization's product is compared with similar products and potential customers give their feedback about which product they prefer

TEST MARKETING

Test marketing refers to actually trying out a product on a representative group of potential consumers and assembling their responses into a comprehensive and useful collection of data, which will be used to devise strategies to market the product or, if necessary, modify the product to remedy deficiencies.

CONSUMER MARKETS

Consumer markets are defined as the sum of all the individuals and households that purchase goods and services for their private consumption and that have the financial resources required to purchase these goods and services.

- By contrast, business-to-business markets consist of all the individuals and households that purchase goods and services intended for use in producing other goods and services or to sell, rent, or lease goods and services to others
- What uniquely distinguishes consumer markets is the end use for the product being sold
- A product or service which is sold for individual consumption is said to be part of a consumer market, while when the same product or service is sold for use by another business, it is said to be part of the business-to-business market

SMALLER MARKET SEGMENTS

Not all products are as universally saleable as, say, McDonald's hamburgers.

- Niche marketing is the process by which an organization sells a product which has appeal in a small but profitable segment of the market. Such a niche may consist of a variety of locations, each with specific characteristics; or it may be a cultural or ethnic group with specific tastes
- Another approach to reaching smaller market segments is addressed by the concept of one-on-one marketing. Here, a unique package of goods or services is developed for individual consumers. An example could be Dell computers, which provides a whole spectrum of computer-related products and services which can be individually customized for each and every consumer

MARKET SEGMENTATION

Market segmentation refers to ways in which an organization can target specific areas of the global marketplace in which to try to sell its goods or services. For example, geographic segmentation is a process in which specific regions of the country have been identified as being potentially lucrative markets for the goods or services the company is trying to sell.

- Demographic segmentation refers to the process by which different age groups or those of differing educational or income levels are targeted
- Psychographic segmentation occurs when an organization identifies individuals comprising specific lifestyles and targets those groups it feels will be most receptive to its product or service
- The ideal market segmentation strategy targets all those segments which are likely to desire and be capable of purchasing the organization's product

RELATIONSHIP MARKETING

Relationship marketing has developed in part as a response to what have been perceived as the deleterious aspects of mass marketing. In relationship marketing, the orientation becomes more focused on providing custom-made goods and services to individual customers, thus retaining those customers over time.

- Modern technology enables organizations to communicate with individual customers and to tailor their products and services to these customers
- Using relationship marketing, smaller firms can carve out their own niches, and thus can compete effectively for customers with the more traditional, mass-market–oriented larger companies

MASS MARKETING CHARACTERISTICS

Mass marketing came into being following the Industrial Revolution, when technologies enabling mass production came into wide use. Mass marketing refers to developing, distributing, and selling products and services designed to appeal to large groups of people or populations.

- Another way of expressing this idea is to say that in mass marketing; very little market segmentation takes place. Instead, the idea is to sell a product or service to as many consumers as possible

- Mass media has produced many new avenues to pursue mass marketing, especially TV, radio, newspapers, and, more recently, the Internet
- A downside to mass marketing has been the process of depersonalization, in which emphasis on the individual customer gets overlooked in the process of targeting such wide groups

NONPROFIT ORGANIZATIONS MARKETING

Though nonprofit organizations are not oriented to make as much money as possible through the distribution of their products and services, they must attain a minimum level of commercial viability to survive in the marketplace and thus carry on their cause.

- For example, marketing is used in green campaigns to create awareness of the benefits of being environmentally responsible by recycling discarded materials
- State parks may utilize marketing to persuade individuals to contribute to their costs of maintenance or expansion
- Trade groups such as unions and artists' guilds use marketing to advance their interests
- Public schools may employ marketing to support their efforts to deliver quality educational opportunities to the communities they serve

ANALYZING CONSUMER BEHAVIOR

Reference group: A reference group consists of people with characteristics in common whom an individual identifies with and uses as a source of information in the adoption, consciously or unconsciously, of his/her belief system. This belief system comprises assumptions, attitudes, values, or patterns of behavior endorsed by the individuals in the group.

Culture: Culture is that set of assumptions, values, attitudes, and behavior patterns passed on from generation to generation in a given society. Thus, United States culture passes on values commonly described as individualistic, free-thinking, and innovative.

Subculture: A subculture is that set of assumptions, values, attitudes, and behavior patterns that can be associated with an ethnic/racial identity, religious identification, or even age group to which an individual belongs.

THREE COMPONENTS OF A MARKETING CONCEPT

Customer orientation: This refers to the process of finding out what it is that consumers want and devising products and means of delivering goods and/or services to satisfy those desires. Note that customer orientation concerns itself with fulfilling consumer needs, not in the application of marketing strategies.

Service orientation: This component of the marketing concept refers to attempting to ensure that all members of the organization are working for the same ultimate objective: to deliver customer satisfaction. It is important that service orientation be part of a total organizational effort.

Profit orientation: This component of the marketing concept refers to the necessity of all members of an organization maintaining their focus upon producing those goods and services which will garner for the organization the greatest possible profit, enabling the organization to survive and, if possible, to expand.

INTERNET GROWTH

During the production era, the overriding principle was to produce as many goods as possible and to distribute these goods to the marketplace for sale.

- The 1920s ushered in the selling era, in which the processes of advertising and persuasion were employed to attempt to persuade customers to purchase an organization's products
- Following World War II, in response to the tremendous demand for goods and services, the marketing-concept era began, with its emphasis on being responsive to customers' needs
- As of the 1990s, the customer relationship era has been characterized by the attempt to build customer satisfaction and inspire long-term brand loyalty

PROMOTIONAL MIX ELEMENTS

Advertising: An organization pays for advertising, which is communication focused on one particular product or service, with the objective of bringing the product or service to the attention of potential and current customers. Advertising is typically done with signs, brochures, video/radio commercials, direct mailings, or e-mail messages.

Public relations: A public relations consists of activities implemented in the media to ensure that the company has a strong public image, and includes helping the public to understand the company and its products. Public relations are often considered as one of the primary activities included in promotions.

Personal selling: Personal selling involves the face-to-face promotion and presentation of goods and services to customers. Other aspects of personal selling are the search for new customers and following up after a sale is made.

Sales promotions: Sales promotions are designed to increase consumer demand, stimulate market demand, or improve product availability. Sales promotions involve both media and non-media marketing communications employed for a limited time span.

ADVERTISING

Promotion: Promotion is the tool by which organizations keep their products in the minds of potential customers and in so doing help stimulate demand for the products. Among the elements of a promotional campaign are advertising, publicity, and public relations. Promotion is being done more and more over the Internet these days. Online promotion allows marketers to reach large numbers of potential consumers, especially if it is done on widely visited websites, such as Google and Yahoo. The Internet can also accommodate interactive promotion, whereby consumers can enter into a dialogue with producers and other consumers. Sales promotion is another tool which can keep a product in the minds of potential consumers. Sales promotions consist of such activities as representation at trade shows and exhibitions and use of displays and discount coupons.

Newspaper advertising: because newspapers are most often read in the communities in which they are located, is particularly effective in communicating information about products to local markets. Plus, it is quick and easy to place an ad in a newspaper. The downside is that newspaper ads often compete side-by-side with other ads for similar products. And newspapers are often discarded daily, giving the ad a short life span.

Television: Television advertising has the advantage of engaging the various senses through the use of sight, sound, and motion. Also, television advertisements totally occupy a particular (though short) time span, with no real-time competition from other ads. The main disadvantage of TV ads is that they can be quite expensive to produce and to air.

Internet advertising: Internet advertising has the great advantage of being a very inexpensive way to offer global visibility. Also, Internet advertising is not locked into a particular time slot and can be viewed at any time. The main disadvantage is that the Internet is now packed with advertising, resulting in one's ad getting lost in the crowd.

Retail advertising: Advertising products directly in stores in which the products are found.

Business-to-business advertising: Advertising which one business uses to promote its products to another business.

Institutional advertising: Advertising designed not to sell a product but to enhance a company's image.

Advocacy advertising: Advertising that promotes a particular cause or point of view.

Comparison advertising: Advertising that compares the merits of competing products.

Interactive advertising: Advertising designed to enable customers to choose what types of information they receive.

Advertising Scope

For years, television was the number one venue marketers sought out to advertise their products. But the advent of the VCR and TiVo enabled viewers to fast-forward through commercials or even to skip them entirely, making TV less attractive to advertisers. And video-on-demand poses even greater challenges for marketers attempting to catch consumers' eye.

- As a result, many advertisers have chosen to increase their focus and their resources on online advertising
- Marketers placing their products on the bigger online sites such as Google or Yahoo can reach a huge audience
- And marketers can use the visual and experiential appeal of surfing the Net to entice potential customers to visit their websites, where they can learn more about the company and its products
- Interactive promotion engages potential customers in a dialogue, in which customers can communicate with one another as well as with the seller directly
- Many companies now provide virtual stores, where buyers can examine products and make purchases on the spot.

Product Placement

Product placement is where an advertiser pays to have her product appear in TV shows and movies where the product can be seen by what might be termed a captive audience, and often a very large audience at that.

- Even the movies of such top-flight filmmakers as Steven Spielberg contain many instances of product placement; and television shows now feature product placement as a matter of course (especially reality television)
- The reason this is all possible is that the producers of these TV shows and movies receive occasionally quite large sums of money from the companies placing their products in their shows

- In turn, these companies enter into agreements in which the films are promoted in their business outlets
- McDonald's is famous for cross-promotional agreements of this type

Selling Process Seven Steps

The seven steps in the selling process include the following:

- Prospecting and qualifying. Research potential buyers and select those likely to want a specific product
- Preapproaching. Learn as much as you can about your potential buyers
- Approaching. In essence, devise a way to make a good first impression
- Making the presentation. Identify to the potential customer the reasons why he will want your product
- Answering objections. Try to anticipate negative responses from potential customers, and have a strategy to deal with these responses
- Closing the sale. Have a strategy to move into the phase where the customer is ready to make his purchase
- Following up. Actively seek to learn a customer's impressions of the product, and be prepared to incorporate his view in your future strategy

Global Advertising

Global advertising may appear to be a highly attractive means of promoting a product, as the potential customer base is huge.

- But many experts feel that promotions aimed at specific countries or regions within specific countries may be more effective
- The reason for this is that different countries and regions have different cultural values and languages, as well as different needs and buying habits
- Particularly in the United States, many divergent groups of consumers exist in sufficient numbers to permit specifically targeted promotional efforts
- These groups may be located in specific geographical regions; for example, cities with large Hispanic populations (and as a result many Hispanic restaurants) would be better placed to target hot sauce than regions containing, say, mostly descendants of European populations

Publicity

One of the main components of PR is publicity, which, unlike advertising, is not something a company pays for, thus constituting one of its major advantages as a PR effort.

- Rather, the company utilizes the media to get its message out
- One of the initial steps in introducing a product to the public is to issue press releases
- Press releases must be developed with great care, as the company seeks to effectively attract the interest of the media, so that the media will want to publish this information
- In addition to being free, publicity has the added advantage of reaching people who might not read an advertisement or watch a commercial for the product
- For example, the product might be featured in a newspaper or TV news story

Publicity Disadvantage

The main disadvantage of publicity is that the company has no control over how or when the media may present the information the company wishes to convey.

- The media may choose to simply discard the story or may even change it in a way that is less positive than the organization may want

PR Campaign

Public relations is the process in which an organization manages the communications between the company and its customers. The main goal of PR is to create exposure for a company and its products. The three main steps in a PR campaign are:

- Listening to the public. Another term for this effort is market research, in which public attitudes are evaluated
- Changing policies and procedures. An organization must respond to the information it receives in the first step and must adapt and evolve its methods of operation to best make use of this information
- Informing the public that you are responsive to their needs. The public must know that you have their interests in mind, and you need to communicate this to them

Sampling, the Promotional Tool

Most often used when introducing a new product, sampling is a promotional technique whereby a company offers consumers a small sample of its product free of charge or at a substantial price break.

- It is often the case that customers will be reluctant to purchase a new product before having been given an opportunity to see it or try it out
- A common manifestation of sampling occurs in the neighborhood grocery store, where representatives of the company set up in-store displays where customers can get a small taste of the product being introduced
- Word-of-mouth in the traditional sense is not considered one of the major promotional tools
- But the advent of the Internet has changed that, in that a great number of potential customers can be easily reached
- Anything that gets people to talk or communicate to one another about a product may be a good expression of word-of-mouth promotion
- The idea is to get more people talking about your product so that customers remember it when they shop

Sales Promotions

Sales promotions are promotional tools designed to incentivize customers to purchase a company's products and to increase dealer interest by employing media and nonmedia marketing communication for a predetermined, limited time.

- Sales promotions can be used internally to stimulate enthusiasm within the company about a product and are typically directed at salespeople and other customer-contact personnel
- External sales promotions are geared toward generating enthusiasm among dealers and distributors of the product

Some examples of sales promotions are:

- Coupons
- Discounts
- Bonuses
- Premiums
- Contests
- Sweepstakes

World Marketing Global Influence

The term blog is short for "web log" and refers to an online journal or diary.

- A blog is usually maintained by an individual and is updated regularly with commentary, descriptions of events, or other material such as graphics or video
- A blog looks just like a webpage but is much easier to create and modify, which can be done by adding images, text, or links to other websites
- Blogs have wildly proliferated of late; it is estimated that there over 30 million blogs currently active on the Internet, and 40,000 new ones appear each day
- Many blogs provide commentary or news on a particular subject, and this is where they come into play as a technique that can be exploited by marketers
- If they can create positive buzz about a product among bloggers, the promotional campaign can rapidly expand and reach a great many potential customers

Viral Marketing

Viral marketing is a type of word-of-mouth promotion where a company pays people to spread positive things about its product across a wide range of venues—especially the Internet.

- One strategy is to hire people to enter Internet chat rooms and to talk up the product to others in the chat room
- Payment for this service is often provided in the form of free merchandise, such as T-shirts or free tickets to entertainment or sports events
- Another way viral marketing works is to offer consumers commissions for getting acquaintances and others to go to the company's website
- Referrals and positive testimonials also play a part in a viral marketing campaign, and companies often encourage customers to provide them

Finance

Finance is defined as that business process whereby firms acquire funds to conduct their business, as well as manage those funds in the most productive manner. Firms need to determine ways to raise the funds or the capital to pay for any kind of expenditure.

Without a sound financial plan, a firm has little chance of survival, much less success. That's where financial management comes in. Financial management is the process by which a firm monitors its resources in a manner that enables it to accomplish its goals and objectives.

Among the activities comprising financial management are:

- Preparing budgets
- Financial reporting
- Collecting accounts receivable

- Analyzing cash flow
- Planning for expenditures
- Managing risk
- Obtaining insurance

PUSH STRATEGIES

A prime concern for any organization wanting to sell a product is the process of moving that product from producers to consumers.

- A push strategy is that effort which is designed to encourage wholesalers and retailers to stock and sell the product using such merchandising techniques as advertising and sales promotions
- When a push strategy is effective, customers will see the product when they enter the retail outlet and, hopefully, purchase it

PULL STRATEGY

Similar to a push strategy is a pull strategy, the difference being that with a pull strategy the promotional effort is focused upon consumers, in the hope that they will request product from retailers. When a pull strategy is effective, retailers will become aware of demand for the product and will order it from the wholesaler. Clearly, television is a prime venue for utilizing pull strategy.

BUDGET TYPES

The three types of budgets commonly established in a firm's financial plan are:

- *Capital budget.* A capital budget concerns itself with a company's plan to finance long-term outlays, such as for fixed assets like facilities and equipment. The capital budget involves evaluating which long-term projects are worth undertaking by analyzing their cash flows and rates of return
- *Cash budget.* A cash budget is used to estimate a company's cash receipts and expenditures. In other words, it is an estimate of the company's cash inflows and outflows. This estimate is used by managers to assess how the firm will handle borrowing, debt repayment, and day-to-day operating expenses
- *Operating budget.* Generally, the most comprehensive budget a company prepares, the operating budget consolidates the company's other budgets and uses them to summarize the company's proposed financial activities. Basically, it is a detailed projection of all estimated income and expenses during a specified period, usually one year

FINANCIAL PLANNING STEPS

Forecasting financial needs; short-term forecasting is used to project revenues, costs, and expenses over a span of a year or less. This type of forecasting is crucial to the day-to-day operation of a firm. Long-term forecasting is used to project these same revenues, costs, and expenses over a longer time span, often five or ten years

Developing budgets to meet financial needs; simply, a budget is a financial plan. A budget is derived from a firm's financial statements and identifies the firm's expected revenues. The types of budgets which compose a firm's financial plan generally include:

- A capital budget
- A cash budget
- An operating budget

Financial controls are the tools by which a firm compares its actual revenues, costs, and expenses with the projections made in its budget. Financial controls enable management to evaluate a firm's performance against its expectations and to take corrective action if those expectations are not met.

Acquiring Inventory

A company is obligated to meet its inventory requirements, and if it does not, this will severely hamper its efforts to attract and keep its customers. However, this can be a very expensive proposition, involving a significant expenditure of the company's funds.

- A well-crafted inventory system will greatly assist a company in managing its funds, retaining and expanding its customer base, and thus maximizing its profit

Capital Expenditures

Capital expenditures are often defined as major outlays of funds in such concrete assets as real estate, structures, and equipment; and in such intangible assets as intellectual property rights, like patents and copyrights.

- Acquiring these major assets often involves spending large sums of money and thus must be the subject of intense scrutiny to determine if these outlays make strategic sense

Operating Funds

Day to day needs: The day-to-day needs of the business include such requirements as:

- Meeting payroll obligations
- Making payments to lenders
- Making interest payments
- Paying such bills as utility bills and phone bills

Clearly, operating funds are required for these services, without which a business will quickly come to a standstill.

- Paying these obligations too soon deprives the company of the interest it would receive on these funds if they were in some investment vehicle
- It is in a company's best interest to keep these daily cash needs to a minimum, in order to free up funds for other, more crucial business needs

Credit operations: Credit operations are also crucial for a business in order to keep existing customers satisfied and to attract new ones.

- If a company were to deny available credit to creditworthy customers, the firm would quickly have trouble competing in the marketplace with its competitors
- Offering credit to customers, however, has the disadvantage of tying up the company's cash assets in accounts receivable from the customers who have purchased its products on credit

Short-Term Loans

Unsecured loan: A loan, in which the borrower is not required to offer any collateral, thus is not backed by any specific assets. Typically available only to highly regarded customers, this is the most difficult type of loan to obtain.

Line of credit: A type of unsecured loan in which a bank provides the borrower with access to a limited amount of funds to withdraw at her convenience. This type of loan offers the borrower the advantage of not having to apply for a new loan every time money is needed.

Revolving credit agreement: Offered by a bank as a guaranteed line of credit, charging a fee for this service, this is a particularly good source of funds for unexpected cash needs

Loan from a commercial finance company: Often used when a company is unable to obtain a loan from a bank, these arrangements typically come with higher interest rates, due to the inherent risk involved

Debt Financing

Debt financing refers to raising funds through any of a variety of borrowing options, such as lines of credit and unsecured loans. These funds will have to be repaid according to the terms of the loan.

Equity Financing

Equity financing refers to a method of financing in which a company issues shares of its stock and receives money in return. Acquiring this money may result in a company relinquishing a significant percentage of the business to the lender.

Short-Term Financing

Short-term financing typically refers to obtaining funds that will be needed for a period of a year or less.

Long Term Financing

Long-term financing, by contrast, refers to obtaining funds that will be needed for a period longer than a year, often two to ten years.

Commercial Paper

Commercial paper is issued by companies to meet short-term financing needs.

- When a company needs funds for a short span of time and seeks lower interest rates than it can get from its bank, commercial paper is typically the route it takes
- Commercial paper calls for the payment of money at a specified date, usually within 2 to 270 days
- Note that commercial paper is unsecured, consisting of promissory notes in amounts of $100,000 and up
- Because it is unsecured, commercial paper is typically available to only large companies with excellent credit
- For them, it is an ideal way to obtain short-term funds quickly, and at an interest rate lower than that charged by a commercial bank

Factoring

Factoring is one means for a company to obtain short-term funds. Essentially, factoring can be described as the process by which a company sells its accounts receivable for cash. Here's how it works:

- A company has sold a large quantity of its product to its customers on credit
- This activity increases the company's number of accounts receivable

- But a certain number of these customers may be late in paying their bills, resulting in the company having a significant amount of money which it is due to receive
- In this case, a bank or other financial institution acts as a factor, agreeing to buy the company's accounts receivable for cash, but at a discount
- Then, the factor collects and keeps the money that was owed the company upon collecting the accounts receivable

BOND

A bond is another type of long-term debt obligation, in which a company issues what are in essence IOUs with a promise to repay the debt in a specified period of time.

- Bonds are often resorted to when a company is unable to obtain long-term financing from a financial institution
- Bonds are also issued by the government, which happens to be the main competitor to those bonds issued by private enterprise or a public enterprise like a utility
- Bonds can be either secured or unsecured
- Secured bonds are backed by some kind of collateral, such as a physical asset like real estate or equipment
- Unsecured bonds, called debenture bonds, are backed by only the creditworthiness or the reputation of the bond issuer

LONG-TERM LOAN

Long-term loans are generally offered to firms which have developed a strong relationship with a bank, an insurance company, a pension fund, or a commercial finance company.

- The term of long-term loans can range from 3 to 7 years but can range to terms of 15 or even 20 years
- Long-term loans are typically more expensive, in the sense of having higher interest rates, than short-term loans, generally because the amounts involved tend to be significantly higher
- Most long-term loans require collateral, which can be in the form of stock or physical assets such as equipment or real estate
- Long-term loans require the borrower to sign a term-loan agreement, which sets out the term of the loan and the interest rate which the borrower will pay

LEVERAGE CONCEPT

Leverage is that process by which companies raise desired funds by borrowing. Such companies are said to be leveraged.

- The leveraged companies then uses the borrowed funds to invest in another financial enterprise, in the hope that the return on this investment will be greater than the rate of interest it must pay on the loan
- If a business is borrowing large sums of money, it is at much greater risk of failure or bankruptcy if it is not able to make required payments on its debt. Or it may be unable to find institutions or individuals willing to lend to it in the future
- However, leverage is not necessarily a bad thing, as it can increase shareholders' return on their investment
- Finally, there are certain tax advantages associated with borrowing

Obtaining Equity Financing

The following three methods of obtaining equity financing:

- *Equity financing by selling stock*: Often a company arrives at a point where it needs funds above and beyond those available through debt financing. One of the most common ways to obtain these funds is through selling partial ownership in the company in the form of stock. Before a company can offer stock for sale, it must meet various requirements set out by the SEC (Securities and Exchange Commission), as well as certain state agencies
- *Equity financing from retained earnings*: This is the practice of reinvesting the profits a company earns back into the company, in the form of what are called retained earnings. The great advantage of this type of financing is that the company will not have to make interest payments or pay dividends to stockholders on the funds reinvested
- *Equity financing from venture capital*: Venture capital is typically needed when a company is starting up and has few assets and no reputation upon which to attain loans from a bank or other financial institution

Issuing Stock Advantages

One of the advantages of issuing stock is that since stockholders are in essence owners of the business, they never have to be repaid.

- Another is that although some companies choose to pay dividends to their stockholders, there is no legal obligation to do so, enabling income to be reinvested in the company to provide for other financing needs
- Issuing stock contributes to a company's overall worth, since stock is not a form of debt which the company must pay back

Issuing Stock Disadvantages

Disadvantages of issuing stock include the fact that a company doing so relinquishes some control of its self-management to stockholders, who become partial owners of the company and have a right to vote on who sits on the company's board of directors

- Dividends are not tax deductible, but rather are paid from a company's after-tax profits. Plus, since stockholders are partial owners, management might have to make concessions to them which they would otherwise be disinclined to make

Issuing Bonds Advantage

One advantage of issuing bonds is that bondholders are not owners, so management maintains control of the company, rather than relinquishing control to outside investors.

- Another is that the interest paid to bondholders is tax deductible to the company issuing the bond, offering the company a way to limit its tax liabilities
- Bonds are an effective means for a company to obtain funding, and when bonds are paid off in full, the debt disappears
- Bonds can be convertible to common stock

Bond Disadvantages

Disadvantages to bonds include:

- A bond is in essence a type of borrowing, which increases a company's debt and can make the firm appear weaker financially
- A company issuing bonds must pay interest to bondholders or risk legal action against the company
- Importantly, the face value of the bond must be repaid upon maturity, risking the possibility of cash flow difficulties

Stock Exchange

A stock exchange is an organized market where members buy and sell shares of common stock and stock equivalents. In the United States, the SEC (Securities and Exchange Commission) regulates the stock exchanges, but investors can also purchase and sell shares of stock on foreign exchanges.

NYSE

The New York Stock Exchange (NYSE), commonly referred to as the Big Board, is a group of 2,800 typically very large companies and is the largest such exchange in the United States. The total market value of the NYSE is about $20 trillion.

NYSE MKT

One of the world's foremost equities exchanges is the NYSE MKT, or NYSE MKT LLC, formerly the American Stock Exchange (AMEX) and, after that, NYSE Amex Equities. It is designed for small-capital companies. Like the NYSE it handles stocks of companies from all over the United States. The regulations under which the NYSE MKT operates are typically somewhat more lenient than those governing the NYSE, so it therefore has a larger representation of stock issued by smaller companies.

NASDAQ

The National Association of Securities Dealers Automated Quotations (NASDAQ) differs from the NYSE in that it is not a floor-based exchange; rather, all transactions on NASDAQ take place over a network of computers and telephones.

Preferred Stock

Preferred stock has characteristics similar to those of both bonds and stocks and is often referred to as a hybrid.

- Preferred stock is similar to bonds in that dividends are based upon what is called a par value and return a fixed, unfluctuating rate of return upon this value
- Owners of preferred stock are promised a fixed annual dividend on their base investment
- These dividends are paid to preferred stockholders before common stockholders are paid their dividends; and in the event of a company's liquidation, preferred stockholders take precedence over common stockholders
- Preferred stockholders have no voting rights in the company

Common Stock

Common stock is the most fundamental type of ownership in a company.

- Common stockholders have voting rights in the company and thus have some influence over its governance
- Common stockholders share in the company's profits through the payment of dividends
- Common stockholders sometimes have what is termed preemptive rights, enabling them to have first rights to purchase any new shares of common stock the company offers

Growth Stocks

Growth stocks are stocks which are expected to produce earnings higher than other stocks in its industry or in the overall market. As a result, growth stocks typically pay little or no dividends.

Income Stocks

Income stocks are a stock with a history of paying consistently high dividend yield on investment

Blue Chip Stocks

Blue-chip stocks are stocks in what are generally perceived to be high-value companies, such as IBM and GE. These stocks generally sell at a high price, due to public confidence in their consistent record of steady earnings

Penny Stocks

Penny stocks are stocks that sell for less than $1.00 a share, though some analysts put this number at $5.00 a share. Penny stocks are generally considered highly risky investments, as the companies offering penny stock are frequently in high-risk industries and have only a few million dollars in assets.

Investment Options

The five principal considerations to take into account when seeking investment options:

- *Risk*: The chance that the value of an investment will decrease in the future. The rule of thumb is: The greater the risk, the greater the reward—in the form of higher dividends or higher interest returned on the principal invested
- *Yield*: The anticipated rate of return on an investment, whether it be in the form of dividends or interest, over a period of time, typically one year
- *Duration*: The span of time an investor's money is committed to an investment, as in a bond with a specified date of maturity upon which the bond's face value must be repaid
- *Liquidity*: A measure of how quickly the funds put into an investment can be turned back into cash
- *Tax consequences*: Different types of investments are treated differently by the Internal Revenue Service, and must be considered when choosing where to invest

DIVERSIFYING INVESTMENTS

Diversification refers to the practice of purchasing a number of different investment vehicles, such as stocks, bonds, and real estate, with the objective of minimizing risk should one or more of them fail or lose value.

- Volatility in a single or a limited number of asset classes is mitigated because not all asset classes increase or decrease in value at the same time or at the same rate
- Diversification serves to minimize both the upside and the downside potential or the investor's portfolio, allowing for more consistent performance under a wide range of market conditions
- Other terms for a diversification strategy are portfolio strategy and allocation model

MUTUAL FUNDS

A mutual fund raises money from shareholders, pools that money, and then, according to the staged objectives of the fund, invests it in a group of assets like stocks, money market instruments, or bonds.

- When shareholders invest in a mutual fund, they receive an equity position in the fund and, for all practical purposes, in the underlying securities
- Generally, investors are free to sell their shares at any time they so desire, although the price of a share in the fund will fluctuate, depending on the current value of the underlying securities
- A key advantage to an investor entering a mutual fund is that he can purchase most funds directly, thus avoiding having to pay fees or commissions
- Mutual funds offer liquidity and convenience

BOND QUOTATIONS, STOCK QUOTATIONS, AND MUTUAL FUND QUOTATIONS

The following types of information can be found in bond quotations, stock quotations, and mutual fund quotations:

- The percent a stock's price has changed for the year to date (YTD)
- The stock's highest and lowest selling prices over the previous 52 weeks
- The company's name and its stock symbol
- The stock's annual dividend yield as a percentage of the price per share
- The price to earnings ratio (P/E), which is the price per share divided by the earnings per share
- The number, in 100s, of shares of stock in the company which were traded that day
- The net change in the price of a stock from one day to the next

COMMODITIES

The term commodities refer to physical substances such as coffee, pork bellies, oil, wheat, or metals, which are interchangeable with other physical substances of the same type.

- Commodities are an inherently risky investment vehicle and can result in handsome profits for investors who are skilled in using this type of investment
- A commodity exchange is a market organized around the buying and selling of commodities
- A commodity exchange operates in a manner quite similar to a stock exchange
- A commodity exchange is considered a public entity, because any investor who wishes to trade in commodities can do so through any of its member firms

- Futures markets revolve around the buying and selling of commodities, bonds, or currency at a specific price on a specified future date
- In other words, futures contracts represent a pledge to conduct a certain transaction at a future date
- Futures trading is a zero-sum game, in which dollars lost by one party in a transaction are equal to the profits earned by the opposite party

Federal Reserve System

The Federal Reserve System (the Fed) is that government body which is charged with monetary policy in the United States. Its objective is to utilize correct monetary policy in order to prevent the US economy from growing too quickly or too slowly. The five major portions of the Fed are:

- The Board of Governors, the governing body of the Federal Reserve System, which supervises the 12 Federal Reserve Banks
- The Federal Open Market Committee (FOMC), the policymaking body of the Federal Reserve System, consisting of 12 members, who set interest rates and credit policy for the Fed
- Twelve Federal Reserve Banks
- Three advisory councils
- Member banks of the system

The Dow

The Dow Jones Industrial Average (the Dow) is the most widely used indicator of the overall condition of the stock market and consists of the average cost of 30 actively traded blue chip stocks, primarily industrial stocks, selected by the editors of the Wall Street Journal, which is published by Dow Jones & Company.

- In a nutshell, the editors of the Journal compute the sum total of all the 30 selected stocks and divide the result by the number of stocks in the index
- The Dow is designed to give an indication of the direction of the broader market over time
- New stocks are substituted for old ones when the editors of the Journal feel the situation is warranted
- A criticism of the Dow is that the sample of only 30 companies is too small to provide an accurate statistical evaluation of the market

Commercial Bank

Commercial banks are profit-seeking institutions that service two types of customers: depositors and borrowers.

- Commercial banks receive deposits from individuals and corporations and hold these deposits in checking and savings accounts; they then use these funds to make loans to borrowers
- Commercial banks make a profit when the revenue generated by the loans they provide is greater than the sum of the amount they pay out in interest to depositors and their operating expenses

Demand Deposit

Demand deposit is the technical name for a checking account. Banks typically charge checking account holders a service fee for processing their checks.

TIME DEPOSIT

Time deposit is another name for a savings account.

CERTIFICATE OF DEPOSIT

Certificate of deposit is in essence, an interest-earning savings account which pays its interest at its stated date of maturity.

LOANS

Loans are offered in a variety of types to its institutional and individual customers, generally contingent on the customer's perceived ability to repay the loan.

RESERVE REQUIREMENT

Reserve requirement is the legally mandated amount of money and liquid assets that Federal Reserve System member banks must keep, either in cash of in non-interest-bearing accounts at the local Federal Reserve district bank, expressed in the form of a percentage of their checking and savings accounts.

OPEN MARKET OPERATIONS

Open-market operations are actions of the Domestic Trading Desk of the Federal Reserve Bank of New York to purchase and sell government bonds. Open-market operations are the tool by which the Fed increases or decreases the money supply.

DISCOUNT RATE

Discount rate is one of two interest rates set by the Fed. The discount rate is the interest rate charged by the Fed for member banks to borrow money from it.

EFT

Electronic funds transfer (EFT) is the transfer of funds from one place to another by a computer system. EFT systems offer a much faster and more efficient means of moving money from one place to another than the traditional method of paper checks. In EFT systems, many types of transactions can take place, such as credit card purchases and delivery of Social Security payments

ECC

Electronic check conversion (ECC) is the process by which a traditional paper check is converted into an electronic transaction at a cash register (also called a point-of-sale terminal)

DEBIT CARDS

Debit cards perform much the same function as paper checks. They withdraw funds from a checking account at the time of purchase.

SMART CARDS

Smart cards are an electronic transfer tool that combines the functions of credit cards, debit cards, phone cards, driver's licenses, and more. Smart cards, equipped with a microprocessor, thus store a whole variety of information, giving them great flexibility.

Pension Funds

A pension fund consists of money collected by a nonprofit corporation of a union from employers, employees, and workers.

- This money is then invested in securities and other assets and pays benefits to the members of the fund upon their retirement
- Due to the fact that pension funds are designed to benefit retirees, the investment strategies that a pension fund employs are generally considered to be conservative in nature, often limiting itself to such investment vehicles as government bonds or life insurance annuities
- Recently, however, to keep pace with other, higher-yielding investments, pension funds have pursued more aggressive, and thus risky, investment vehicles in order to achieve higher rates of return
- Pension funds often amass huge sums of money; and because of these enormous resources, pension funds hold considerable influence over the investment community

Accounting Aspects

Financial accounting: concerned with obtaining financial information for people outside the organization

Managerial accounting: concerned with obtaining financial information for managers within the organization

Annual report: a yearly statement summarizing a company's financial condition and progress

Public accountant: professional who provides accounting services for individuals or corporate institutions for a fee

Certified public accountant: either a private or a public accountant who has passed a series of tests conducted by the American Institute of Certified Public Accountants

Accounting

Accounting can be defined as the bookkeeping methods invoked to provide a financial record of business transactions. Specifically, accounting is the process of recording, classifying, summarizing, and interpreting financial events and transactions in order to provide management with the interpreted data necessary to make sound business decisions. Some of the users of accounting may be:

- Government tax agencies, for tax returns
- Government regulatory agencies, for reports they deem necessary
- Financial analysts, for financial statements, including such information as income, cash flow, and debts
- Corporate management, for financial statements and financial reports internal to the company

Managerial Accounting

Managerial accounting is the internal process by which management personnel of an organization gather information and analyses within the organization to aid in management's decision-making process.

- Among the activities involved in managerial accounting are measuring and reporting on costs of production; analyzing whether specific departments are operating within their expected budget limitations; preparing budgets; and devising legal strategies to minimize tax obligations
- By contrast, financial accounting is intended to provide information to parties outside the organization
- Managerial accounting is also known as cost accounting

Auditing

The purpose of auditing is to add credibility to an organization's management assertion that its financial statements are relevant, accurate, complete, and fairly presented and that they accurately represent the organization's position and performance to the firm's stakeholders and other interested parties, like tax authorities, banks, regulators, suppliers, customers and employees.

- Audits are designed to detect missing or false information, whether caused by intentional action such as fraud or by simple oversight or miscalculation
- Audits may be conducted by qualified professionals within a firm, called private auditors, or by outside professionals, called public auditors

Double-Entry Bookkeeping

Double-entry bookkeeping is a process whereby all transactions are recorded in two different locations, to reduce the chance of error.

Trial Balance

Trial balance is a summary of the financial information in the account ledgers, intended to ensure accuracy of the information.

Balance Sheet

Balance sheet is a financial statement which provides the firm's financial condition on a specific date.

Income Statement

Income statement is a financial statement which summarizes incoming revenues against the cost of goods and expenses over a specific time span, thus showing the firm's profit or loss during that span.

Statement of Cash Flows

Statement of cash flows is a financial statement which summarizes money coming into or flowing out of the company as cash receipts and cash payments. The six steps in the accounting cycle:

- Analyzing documents and records, such as invoices and travel expenses
- Recording transactions in journals
- Posting journal entries to the ledger
- Taking a trial balance

- Preparing financial statements
- Analyzing financial statements

Revenue

Revenue is defined as the total value a firm receives for the goods it sells and the services it renders.

Cost of Goods Sold

Cost of goods sold represents how much the firm pays for the raw materials and labor to make its product or deliver its service.

Gross Profit

Gross profit equals revenue minus the cost of goods sold.

Operating Expenses

Operating expenses are the costs the firm incurs in the course of operating its business, such as rent, payroll, and supplies.

Net Income

Net income before taxes equals gross profit minus operating expenses.

Taxes

Taxes, of course, are the state, federal, and occasionally city assessments a firm pays to the government.

Net Income (or Loss)

Net income (or loss) equals net income before taxes minus taxes.

Accounts Payable

Accounts payable are current liabilities in which the firm owes money for merchandise or services bought on credit but not paid for in full—in simple terms, a bill that a firm hasn't yet paid in full

Notes Payable

Notes payable are short or long-term loans a firm has obtained from a bank or other source of financing which the firm has promised to repay by a specific date.

Intangible Assets

Intangible assets are long-term assets with no actual physical form, typically intellectual property assets such as trademarks, copyrights, and patents.

Fixed Assets

Fixed assets are long-term assets such as property, buildings, equipment, and other such tangible parts of an organization.

Bonds Payable

Bonds payable are long-term liabilities which will have to be repaid and which result from the firm's having been loaned money and having issued bonds in return.

Cash Flow Problems

One way a firm can get into cash flow problems is by purchasing more and more goods on credit while simultaneously selling more and more of its own products or services on credit.

Thus, even if the firm has sold a great quantity of its goods or services, it has received little cash for these sales. And having exhausted its available credit with its lenders, the company is now in a position where its lenders may refuse to lend the firm the funds necessary to pay for a crucial bill, say, to one of its suppliers. Suddenly, the firm's consequent inability to pay its debts may well force the company into bankruptcy.

Cash Flow

Cash flow is a measure of a company's health and is crucial to the effective functioning of the company. Poor cash flow analysis can result in a company selling lots of its product and making a hefty profit but still being in danger of going under, due to an improper or incomplete accounting of the difference between the amount of cash coming in and going out of the company.

Cash Flow Analysis

Basically, cash flow analysis is an accounting of the changes in the company's financial position which occur as a result of expenses related to the company's operations, investments, and financing, as explained below:

- Operations consist fundamentally of the costs of operating the business, including rent, salaries, equipment, insurance, and utilities
- Investments consist of the cash a firm uses in its enterprises, as well as the cash provided by these enterprises in the form of interest and dividends
- Financing refers to the cash generated through issuing debt or to the cash with which the company repays debts or pays out dividends on its stock

Liquidity and Liquidity Ratios

Liquidity is defined as how quickly and how cheaply an asset can be converted into cash.

- Money in the form of cash is the asset with the highest liquidity
- Liquidity ratios are, in their simplest definition, a firm's total dollar value of its cash and marketable securities divided by its current liabilities
- A firm's liquidity ratios are of particular interest to a firm's short-term creditors, as liquidity ratios typically reflect a firm's ability to pay off its short-term debts
- In general, the higher the value of the ratio, the greater likelihood the firm possesses the means to cover its short-term debts

Financial Ratios

Financial ratios can be defined as the organizing and interpreting of relationships among data found in a firm's financial statements.

- Financial ratios are often used to compare the performance of a firm against other firms' within the same industry in the key areas of liquidity, leverage, profitability, and general business activity

- Financial ratios consist of quantitative analyses, in which ratios calculated from the firm's current numbers are compared with those of previous years, with those of other firms, or even with the economy as a whole
- Understanding and correctly interpreting these ratios are a significant part of attempting to attain a sound financial picture of the firm's performance

LEVERAGE RATIOS

Leverage ratios are a measure of the degree to which a company depends upon borrowed funds. Another way to put it is:

- Leverage ratios are those ratios which measure the extent to which fixed-term obligations are used to finance its assets
- The idea is to identify when a firm enters territory in which it has taken on such a significant quantity of debt that it could experience difficulties repaying its lenders or meeting its obligations to stockholders

DEBT TO OWNERS' EQUITY RATIO

The debt to owners' equity ratio is obtained by calculating the firm's total liabilities divided by its total shareholders' (owners') equity. Any resulting number over 100 percent indicates that the firm has more debt than equity, and thus may appear risky to some lenders or investors

LIQUIDITY RATIOS

The current ratio, which can be found on a firm's balance sheet, is simply a number which is calculated by dividing the firm's current assets by its current liabilities.

- If the result is a number greater than 2—that is, the firm's current assets are at least twice the value of its current liabilities—the company is generally considered to be in good short-term financial health
- Contrariwise, if the firm's assets are less than its liabilities, the firm may well have trouble meeting its short-term obligations

ACID TEST RATIO

The acid-test ratio (or quick ratio), which can also be found on a firm's balance sheet, is the number which is calculated by dividing the firm's marketable securities such as stocks and bonds—but not including the firm's inventories—by its current liabilities.

- This ratio is considered more stringent than the current ratio, as it considers only those assets which can be quickly converted into cash

PROFITABILITY RATIOS

The following three ratios that comprise profitability ratios:

- *Earnings per share* (EPS): This indicator of a firm's profitability reflects that portion of the firm's profit which is allocated to each outstanding share of common stock. In other words, EPS = Net income ÷ n outstanding shares of common stock
- *Return on sales* (ROS): This indicator of a firm's operational efficiency provides a comparison with competitors to judge the firm's success in generating income from its sales. ROS is calculated: ROS = Net income ÷ Net sales

- *Return on equity* (ROE): This indicator of a firm's profitability reflects how much profit the firm creates using the money that has been invested by shareholders. ROE = Net income after tax ÷ Total shareholders' equity

Profitability

Profitability, simply put, is the measure of a firm's ability to generate net income on a consistent basis.

- Profitability ratios, otherwise known as performance ratios, are used to assess a firm's ability, through the use of its various resources, to generate earnings as compared with its expenses and other relevant costs over a specific span of time
- As a general rule, having a higher profitability ratio than a competitor's is a good indication that the company is doing well
- And profitability ratios are often a good measure of the effectiveness of management's performance

Product Offer Components

12 components of a total product offer are:

- Price
- Brand name
- Convenience
- Package
- Store surroundings
- Service
- Internet access
- Buyer's past experience
- Guarantee
- Speed of delivery
- Image created by advertising
- Reputation of producer

Inventory Turnover Ratio

The inventory turnover ratio is the accounting liquidity ratio which measures the speed at which a firm's inventory moves through the firm and is converted into sales.

- It is a measure of the average number of times the inventory is sold during a specified time period
- Also known as the turnover ratio, it is used to maximize the efficiency with which the firm manages its inventory, on the principle that it is preferable to sell inventory rather than incur the costs of storing this inventory in its warehouse
- The inventory turnover ratio is calculated: Inventory turnover ratio = Cost of goods sold ÷ Average inventory

Consumer Goods and Services

Consumer goods and services are those products whose intended customers are individuals and groups of individuals who will themselves consume or otherwise make use of the product being offered. Some examples of consumer goods are food items and consumer electronics (such as TVs and computers); examples of consumer services are duplicating facilities and laundromats.

Industrial Goods and Services

By contrast to consumer goods and services, industrial goods and services (sometimes referred to as business-to-business, or B2B, goods) are those products which are used in the production of other products and are sold in the traditional B2B marketplace. An example of an industrial good is office supplies; an example of a service is maintenance of a company's existing equipment.

Product Line

Product line is a group of complementary products made by a specific manufacturer which occupy a similar market or share physically similar characteristics. Each product in the line utilizes the same distribution channels and manufacturing facilities. An example could be McDonald's, which has developed a product line including burgers, fish sandwiches, and chicken sandwiches.

Product Mix

Product mix is complementing a product line is the product mix, which refers to all the products or product lines offered by a firm. For example, Chase Bank offers a product mix consisting of checking accounts, savings accounts, and consumer loans.

Product Differentiation

Product differentiation is what marketers strive to achieve for their products, in which there is a real or at least a perceived individuality which contrasts or stands out from other similar products made by other firms.

Packaging

Packaging has grown in importance lately partially as a result of the Fair Packaging and Labeling Act of 1967/1994, which mandates that labels contain more information than before by which consumers can now better compare the value and quantity of one product with another.

- Many products that were once sold by salespersons are now sold in self-service outlets, making packaging more important than ever

Some of the functions performed by packaging include:

- Attracting the attention of the potential buyer
- Protecting the goods inside the package
- Providing a description of the contents of the package
- Detailing warranty information, including product warnings
- Providing some explanation of the uses and benefits of the goods inside the package

Consumer Goods

Convenience goods and services: This class of consumer goods and services consists of products that a consumer desires to purchase on a regular basis and without having to expend considerable effort. Examples: basic banking services, food snacks.

Shopping goods and services: This class of consumer goods and services consists of products that a consumer will generally buy only after having compared the products with other similar products. Examples include items of apparel, major home appliances, and automobile repair services.

Specialty goods and services: This class of consumer goods and services has a perceived individuality, often associated with a brand name, and generally consists of higher-priced goods such as automobiles, high-end sports equipment, etc.

Unsought goods and services: These are products with which the consumer doesn't generally familiarize herself with, and are often associated with conditions of adversity, such as life insurance.

Brand Equity

Brand equity may be defined as the combination of loyalty, awareness, and perception of product quality that consumers associate with a particular brand name.

Brand Loyalty

Brand loyalty is that component of brand equity with the highest value, as it refers to the degree to which consumers are confident in and committed to a specific brand and are therefore more likely to return to that brand when making a purchase.

- Brand awareness may be characterized by the association a consumer makes in his mind when he thinks about a certain product category and immediately associates this product category with a specific brand name
- Advertising is crucial in establishing brand awareness

Brand Association

Brand association refers to the process whereby a consumer links in his mind a positive association between certain favorable impressions and a specific brand. This is often accomplished by the effective use of symbols and slogans by the seller.

Branding

Branding is the process of assigning a name, a symbol, or a design—or any combination thereof—to a product or service which uniquely distinguishes the product or service from similar products or services provided by competitors. The importance of branding can be seen when certain brand names acquire a special cachet among consumers, who may even substitute the brand name in their minds for the generic product itself, such as Kleenex for a hand tissue.

Dealer Brands

Dealer brands are products that don't have the manufacturer's name attached to them, but rather carry the name of the retailer selling the product instead.

Generic Goods

Generic goods are non-branded products—that is, products that do not have any national or private-label name associated with them—which are generally significantly lower in price than the branded products with which they compete.

Knock Off Brands

Knockoff brands are illegal copies of brand-name goods.

Product Life Cycle

After a product has gone through the six stages of product development, the producer introduces the product into the marketplace. The product life cycle is a theoretical model of how products of a particular type will fare in the marketplace, in terms of sales and profits. The product may fail shortly after its introduction, or it may go on to be a perennial seller. The four phases are:

- *Introduction*. The market-tested product is offered for sale, often with intense advertising support and dealer promotion
- *Growth*. In response to the level of consumer demand and consumer acceptance, the product is improved and the price adjusted accordingly
- *Maturity*. The product may be broken out into different cost strata, in order to satisfy varying market segments
- *Decline*. The product may be eliminated, significantly reduced, or replaced by new products offering superior results to the original

Product Development

Six stages of product development are:

- *Idea generation*, as a response to consumer desires
- *Product screening*, whereby new products are evaluated for potential development
- *Product analysis*, involving cost estimates and sales forecasts
- *Development*, including building prototypes
- *Testing*, where a product idea is introduced to consumers
- *Commercialization*, involving establishing the product with distributors and retailers and developing the sales campaign

Pricing Strategy Objectives

Attaining a return on investment: Since the goal of developing any product is to make a profit, the single ultimate pricing objective of all sellers is to optimize profit.

Building traffic: This is generally part of a firm's short-term pricing strategy, the objective of which is to build a substantial customer base, typically by offering the product at a competitive price.

Gaining greater market share: This aspect of pricing strategy concerns itself with the types of incentives a firm offers its potential customers in order to entice them to buy the firm's products rather than those of its competitors.

Creating an image: Typically the province of higher-priced luxury goods, products designed to enhance the seller's public image are priced relatively high, to give the products an image of exclusivity.

Promoting social objectives: A firm may offer its product at an extremely low price in order to benefit those consumers with little money, and, not coincidentally, in the process enhancing the firm's public profile.

Pricing

Pricing is a crucial component in the marketing and distribution strategy a firm must adopt when bringing a product to market.

- In fact, pricing is often considered the fourth "P" in the marketing mix, in addition to product, place, and promotion
- Importantly, the firm must distinguish between its short-term and its long-term objectives

- When introducing a product into the marketplace, short-term objectives are generally less concerned with immediately attaining a high return on investment, but rather might include attempts to create a large number of sales through offering the product at a highly attractive price relative to its competitors
- Long-term objectives must include attaining a reasonable rate of return on investment, and therefore adjustments must be made to the initial pricing strategy in order to accomplish this end

IMPORTANCE OF PRICING

Pricing is a crucial component in the marketing and distribution strategy a firm must adopt when bringing a product to market.

- In fact, pricing is often considered the fourth "P" in the marketing mix, in addition to product, place, and promotion
- Importantly, the firm must distinguish between its short-term and its long-term objectives
- When introducing a product into the marketplace, short-term objectives are generally less concerned with immediately attaining a high return on investment, but rather might include attempts to create a large number of sales through offering the product at a highly attractive price relative to its competitors
- Long-term objectives must include attaining a reasonable rate of return on investment, and therefore adjustments must be made to the initial pricing strategy in order to accomplish this end

PRODUCT LIFE CYCLE

After a product has gone through the six stages of product development, the producer introduces the product into the marketplace. The product life cycle is a theoretical model of how products of a particular type will fare in the marketplace, in terms of sales and profits. The product may fail shortly after its introduction, or it may go on to be a perennial seller. The four phases are:

- *Introduction*. The market-tested product is offered for sale, often with intense advertising support and dealer promotion.
- *Growth*. In response to the level of consumer demand and consumer acceptance, the product is improved and the price adjusted accordingly.
- *Maturity*. The product may be broken out into different cost strata, in order to satisfy varying market segments.
- *Decline*. The product may be eliminated, significantly reduced, or replaced by new products offering superior results to the original.

PRICING STRATEGIES

Cost-based pricing: The producer carefully accounts for all the various costs (expenses) involved in producing and distributing a product and then uses a target margin of profit by which to set the price of the product.

Demand-based pricing: The opposite strategy to cost-based pricing, demand-based pricing is set by the producer, who, while attempting to satisfy consumer interests, establishes the specific profit margin she hopes to achieve by selling the product, and prices the product accordingly.

Competition-based pricing: Here, the selling firm sets the price of its product by taking into prime consideration the prices set by its competitors. This type of pricing is appropriate when one or more dominant competitors have established a more or less universally accepted pricing framework.

Developing a Pricing Strategy

Attaining a return on investment: Since the goal of developing any product is to make a profit, the single ultimate pricing objective of all sellers is to optimize profit.

Building traffic: This is generally part of a firm's short-term pricing strategy, the objective of which is to build a substantial customer base, typically by offering the product at a competitive price.

Gaining greater market share: This aspect of pricing strategy concerns itself with the types of incentives a firm offers its potential customers in order to entice them to buy the firm's products rather than those of its competitors.

Creating an image: Typically the province of higher-priced luxury goods, products designed to enhance the seller's public image are priced relatively high, to give the products an image of exclusivity.

Promoting social objectives: A firm may offer its product at an extremely low price in order to benefit those consumers with little money, and, not coincidentally, in the process enhancing the firm's public profile.

Skimming Price Strategy

Skimming price strategy is a strategy often used when a new product is introduced to the market, whereby a firm prices the product high in order to try to recover the costs of developing the product.

Penetration Strategy

Penetration strategy is the opposite of a skimming price strategy, whereby when a firm introduces a new product, it is more focused upon quickly capturing a large segment of the market by pricing the product low.

Everyday Low Pricing

Everyday low pricing is a pricing strategy used by huge retailers such as Wal-Mart, whereby prices are set lower than those of their competitors in order to siphon off their customers on an everyday basis

High-Low Pricing

High-low pricing is a strategy often pursued by department stores, which set the everyday price higher than that of outlets employing everyday low pricing but which compensate for this by having many sales during which the prices are lower than their competitors'.

Bundling

Bundling is the practice of selling and offering at a reduced price two or more products together as a package.

Psychological Pricing

Psychological pricing is whereby (in a technique we're all familiar with) an item is made to appear to be less expensive than it actually is, by pricing it at $29.99 rather than $30.00.

Break-Even Point

The break-even point identifies the minimum number of sales a firm must make in order to start making a profit.

- Therefore, break-even analysis (also called cost-volume-profit analysis) is the study of the relationship between costs and revenues, given the firm's total fixed and variable costs
- Total fixed costs are defined as those expenses which stay the same, regardless of the quantity of products produced or sold, such as insurance or rent
- Variable costs are defined as those costs which change according to the quantity of products produced or sold, such as labor and materials
- The break-even point (BEP) is calculated: BEP = total fixed costs ÷ (price of one unit – variable cost of one unit)

CAD

Computer-aided design (CAD) is the process by which computers are used to create and modify graphic images for the design, drafting, and modeling of components, products, and structures.

- CAD replaces the old paper and pencil design mode, enabling product designers to view their ongoing work in three dimensions
- CAD thus significantly increases productivity, as it enables designers to quickly create and modify product designs

CAM

Computer-aided manufacturing (CAM) is the process by which products are physically produced with the aid of computers, often using robots or other such automated production tools.

- Here, a computer program controls the machines that produce the product, eliminating or minimizing the necessity for human intervention, in the process enabling very precise duplication of processes and its consequent reduction of errors

Process Manufacturing

Process manufacturing refers to that phase in producing a product during which physical materials are changed by physical or chemical processes. One example is the process during which the raw material of silicon is converted into the base material utilized in memory chips.

Assembly Process

The assembly process differs from process manufacturing in that no transformation of physical elements is involved. Rather, in the assembly process the various components of a product are put together or assembled, as when the component parts of an automobile are combined.

Continuous Process

Continuous process occurs when products are produced in an ongoing, assembly line type of manner. That is, the product emerging from a continuous process is available anytime the process is in operation.

Intermittent Process

Intermittent process occurs when products are produced on an as-needed basis, often in response to specific customer requests.

MATERIALS REQUIREMENT PLANNING

Materials requirement planning refers to a computer-based information and operations management system which is utilized in the ordering and scheduling of the raw materials, parts, and assembled constructs that are used to complete the production of the finished product. In other words, materials requirement planning ensures that components are available when and where they are needed.

ENTERPRISE RESOURCE PLANNING

Enterprise resource planning is a new variation of materials requirement planning. It is also a computer-based application, one designed to connect all the organizational operations of multiple companies, such as finance, accounting, production, marketing, and distribution, in a single set of data.

- The objective of enterprise resource planning is to facilitate the flow of activity between receiving orders and receiving payment for goods sold
- The importance of a firm's choosing the right facility location, and discuss some of the considerations involved in making such a choice

FACILITY LOCATION

Facility location refers to the precise geographical environment where a firm resides and in which the firm's operations take place.

- In the case of a business which sells its products directly from its place of residence, say, a restaurant, the importance of choosing a suitable location is obvious, as proximity to its customer base is crucial
- But in the case of a firm whose product is sold by external retailers, there are many other issues to consider
- One of the most important considerations for both situations is the availability of competent—and available—labor
- The firm whose product is sold externally may be more concerned with such variables as the region's prevailing wage rate, its state tax rate, and its access to the transportation facilities necessary to get its product to its distributors and retail outlets
- Another consideration is the expense involved in such resources as electricity

PERT

Performance evaluation and review technique (PERT) charts are used to break down a project into tasks, identifying their relationship with one another, their appropriate sequence of events, and the amount of time required to complete each task, along with, ultimately, the minimum amount of time required to finish the entire project.

- An important part of a PERT chart is called critical path, which represents that sequence of events in the production cycle which requires the most time to complete and is thus the most critical

GANTT CHARTS

Gantt charts, named for their developer, Henry L. Gantt, are bar graphs that compare the amount of time scheduled to complete a project and the actual time taken for the project's completion.

- Using Gantt charts, management can track the progress of production and can identify which tasks are taking longer to complete than anticipated

QUALITY CONTROL

Quality control may be defined as the activities utilized in detecting and assessing variability in the process of production, especially as it applies to remedying and preventing errors.

- Early quality control measures were typically implemented by quality control departments at the end of the production line, when products emerged as completed entities
- This orientation meant that additional personnel were required to inspect employees' work, faulty products had to be simply scrapped, and customers receiving faulty products that slipped through the cracks could be alienated and look to other producers
- Today, quality control has evolved to where it is continuously employed in all phases of the production process. Thus, errors which occur early in production can be detected and remedied, before they have become hopelessly integrated into the final product

FORM UTILITY

Form utility is a function typically performed by manufacturers, as opposed to marketing intermediaries.

- Form utility refers to how the marketability of a product can be enhanced by altering its physical makeup
- An example could be changing a powdered form of dishwashing soap to a liquid form more suitable to certain types of equipment

TIME UTILITY

Time utility is one of the functions typically performed by a marketing intermediary.

- It refers to the process by which a product is made more attractive in the marketplace due to its being made available at a convenient time for the consumers who want it

PLACE UTILITY

Place utility is another one of the functions typically performed by a marketing intermediary.

- Place utility refers to the added value which a product attains by nature of the product's close proximity to its customers

MARKETING INTERMEDIARIES

Marketing intermediaries are those individuals and organizations whose function is to facilitate the movement of the raw materials needed to produce products to the producers who make the products, as well as the movement of those products from producers to retail outlets where they will be sold.

- The reason marketing intermediaries are necessary is that manufacturers seldom possess the specific transportation and storage facilities, as well as the relationship-building resources, to perform these functions themselves
- Marketing intermediaries are specialists in a specific link in the chain between production and sale, and thus possess intimate knowledge of their particular area of expertise
- Additionally, marketing intermediaries may reside in geographical areas in which the firm has no physical presence

Wholesale Intermediaries

Wholesale intermediaries are those marketing intermediaries who make business-to-business (B2B) sales.

Merchant Wholesalers

Merchant wholesalers are independent companies or individuals who take title to the goods they handle and assume responsibility for the risks associated with this ownership.

Rack Jobbers

Rack jobbers are those types of wholesalers who fill store racks and shelves with merchandise and then sell that merchandise on consignment.

- That is, they keep title to the merchandise until it is sold to a customer and then they share profit with the retailer

Cash-and-Carry Wholesalers

Cash-and-carry wholesalers generally work with smaller retailers who provide a limited array of products.

Drop Shippers

And drop shippers get orders from retailers and arrange to have products shipped directly from a producer to a buyer.

- While drop shippers own the products they deal with, they are not involved in handling, stocking, or delivering the products

Possession Utility

Possession utility refers to those services performed by marketing intermediaries which enhance a customer's ability to take possession of a product.

- Some of the tasks involved in possession utility include installation, delivery, and even providing credit.

Information Utility

Information utility is the process employed by marketing intermediaries in which they open flows of information between marketing participants.

- For example, a marketing intermediary can recommend websites or government publications to a customer which will enable him to educate himself about the product he seeks to purchase.

Service Utility

Service utility is simply the value added to a transaction as a result of the marketing intermediary providing courteous, fast, and friendly service to the customer.

Electronic Retailing

Electronic retailing involves the selling of goods and services over the Internet.

- All over the world, Internet-based businesses are starting every day, some attaining spectacular success in the absence of physical locations from which to distribute their products
- This is not to say that electronic retailing enables sellers to completely abandon sound traditional business practices, as the failure to maintain effective inventory control, accurate accounting procedures, or responsive customer service can be as detrimental to the success of an online operation as to a traditional one
- In addition to the proliferation of exclusively Internet-related operations, the extremely rapid rise in the use and reach of the Internet has made it imperative for many traditional brick-and-mortar firms to expand into electronic retailing as well, an endeavor often referred to as "brick and click."

Retail Intermediaries

A retail intermediary is, to put it simply, an entity which sells goods and products to the ultimate consumers. Examples of retail intermediaries are Sears, McDonald's, Wal-Mart, and your local stationery store.

The three main types of retail distribution strategies are:

- *Intensive distribution*: The goal of the producer here is to place its product in as many retail outlets as it can. Note that vending machines also count as a type of retail outlet. The products most suited to intensive distribution are ready consumables, such as cigarettes, snacks, and periodicals
- *Selective distribution*: This strategy involves using a limited number of selected retail outlets from which to sell one's product. Larger goods such as appliances and furniture, as well as apparel, are typically sold through selective distribution
- *Exclusive distribution*: Here a firm's product is sold only in a single retail outlet in a specific geographical area. This distribution strategy is typically employed for higher-end products and luxury items

Distribution Systems

Corporate distributions systems: Here all the entities in the organization's distribution chain are owned by a single company. Here, the producer also owns the means of transportation and the retail outlets where its products will be sold.

Contractual distributions systems: Here the producer does not own the retail outlets which will sell its products, but the producer enters into a contractual agreement with the retailer to sell them. Contractual distributions systems can be franchise operations, wholesaler-sponsored chains, or retail cooperatives.

Administered distributions systems: In the absence of a corporate or a contractual distributions system, a producer may enter into an administered distributions system, in which it manages marketing functions such as display and advertising at the retail level.

Supply chains: Also known as value chains, supply chains consist of the entire network of distributors, retailers, storage facilities, and transporters involved in the sale, delivery, and purchase of the producer's product.

Marketing Strategies

Telemarketing: We've all encountered, and occasionally been annoyed by, a telemarketer hawking its product over the telephone. But the fact remains that this can be a legitimate and productive strategy

Vending machines: These machines enable customers to insert a certain amount of cash in the machine and get a product on the spot. The main advantage of vending machines and kiosks is that overhead is very low.

Direct selling: This strategy entails selling one's product to consumers in their own homes or places of work. Years ago, Tupperware was a pioneer in this manner of selling; today Avon and other cosmetic producers are widely recognized.

Multilevel marketing: This is the strategy in which one salesperson recruits a number of other salespersons and receives commissions both from his own sales and from the sales of these persons she has recruited (conversely, each salesperson passes up a portion of her sales to the salesperson who recruited her).

Direct marketing: This strategy encompasses such marketing tools as consumer catalogs and direct mail, in addition to telemarketing and online marketing.

Transportation

Trains, which handle 30 to 40 percent of all goods moved in the United States and are the single largest form of US transportation, are typically used to move large, bulky items such as cars, heavy equipment, lumber, coal, etc. They are a relatively energy-efficient way to transport goods.

Trucks, the second largest form of transportation in the United States, are usually used to transport small shipments of goods to difficult-to-reach locations. Trucks are more affected by changes in energy prices.

Water transportation, an inexpensive but slow means of moving goods, is nevertheless extensively utilized in the transportation of goods overseas. Obviously, proximity of the source and the destination to major waterways is an important consideration.

Pipelines are primarily used to transport water and other liquids and gaseous petroleum products.

Air transportation is the fastest way to get goods from one point to another but has the limitation of being quite expensive.

Transportation Logistics

Transportation logistics may be defined as the management of business operations, specifically the planning and executing of the movement of materials and products from point of origin to point of consumption, where they are made available for sale to consumers. Various types of logistics include:

- *Inbound logistics*: how raw materials get from suppliers to producers
- *Materials handling*: the loading, movement, and unloading of materials both within a warehouse and from the warehouse to the factory

- *Outbound logistics*: the movement of finished products through buyers and ultimately to the consumer
- *Reverse logistics*: the movement of finished products back to the producer, either in the form of returns of faulty products or for recycling

IT CHANGING HOW BUSINESSES OPERATE

One of the main ways in which IT has altered business has to do with the speed at which certain aspects of business can be conducted.

- Where it used to take many hours and the labor of many employees to assemble, organize, and analyze large sets of data, such as a company's payroll system with its profusion of deductions, benefit calculations, job categories, and union and governmental rules, such huge collections of data can be virtually instantaneously accessed with the tremendous speed of today's computer systems, according to parameters selected by managers seeking specific types of information.
- Electronic communications are greatly facilitated by the technological revolution
- E-mail enables instant communication among wide groups of individuals, within an office or around the globe
- IT also breaks down geographical barriers, as more and more businesses conduct their operations and sales efforts over the Internet
- Additionally, the advent of the Internet has produced a revolution in how goods are sold, one example being the way in which entertainment is consumed

DATA AND INFORMATION

Data may be defined as useful factual information which is used as a basis for analysis, reasoning, or calculation (note that data is the plural of the singular datum).

- Data in and of themselves are raw, unorganized, and uninterrupted facts and numbers
- By contrast, information is data which have been organized into useful categories and can then be used as the basis upon which to make business decisions
- Data processing, or DP, was the term used in the 1970s for the business technology involving the organization and interpretation of data
- In the 1980s, data processing came to be known as information systems (IS)
- In this period, IS moved from the remote bowels of a company to the center of its business operations
- Starting in the 1990s, IS shifted to a more sophisticated entity known as information technology (IT)
- Today, the role of IT is central to virtually every aspect of business, from manufacturing to accounting to sales analysis

BUSINESS PROCESS INFORMATION

Business process information is all data collected at point of sale, plus data obtained through all phases of enterprise planning and supply chain and relationship management.

PHYSICAL-WORLD OBSERVATIONS

Physical-world observations are observations obtained through technology relating to where people and objects are located and what they are doing.

Biological Data

Biological data are forms of personal identification, such as biometrics and fingerprints.

Public Data

Public data are free and readily accessible information gleaned from e-mail and the Internet.

Data Including Personal Preferences

Data including personal preferences: data gleaned from the Internet which identifies the sites that users have visited and the products they have bought online.

KT

KT (Knowledge technology), the newest incarnation of information technology, takes raw information and adds a layer of interpretation, which makes the information more relevant and timely.

- BT, a subsequent incarnation of KT, consists of a number of software innovations that scrutinize raw data and draw practical interpretations from it
- These technological advances in essence anticipate the user's goals in collecting data and in effect personalize the data in accordance with the user's intentions
- Utilizing data mining, they also quickly create knowledge databases which previously had to be laboriously constructed, often using supervisory resources
- By quickly making the right information available to the right personnel at the right time, they provide their users with a significant competitive advantage

Data Warehouse

A data warehouse is a repository of a firm's information in which data on specific subjects are organized, standardized, and integrated to facilitate reporting and analytical business functions.

Data Mining

Data mining refers to process by which a firm's IT department sifts through its data warehouse, extracting useful information from these massive stores of data.

- Data mining employs a number of sophisticated technological methodologies, such as artificial intelligence and advanced statistical tools, to search for previously hidden patterns underlying the data
- Data mining has become an increasingly important business tool, used in such diverse business pursuits as marketing, fraud detection, and scientific research
- Note that the effectiveness of data mining is utterly dependent on the reliability and completeness of the data from which it draws its conclusions

Four Characteristics of Information

Quality: This refers to the degree of accuracy and reliability of the information. Errors here can lead to faulty business decisions.

Completeness: An appropriate quantity of information is necessary to make educated conclusions. The corollary can be an overabundance of information, which overburdens the attempt to analyze.

Timeliness: In a rapidly changing business environment, out-of-date information can be as detrimental to success as incorrect or incomplete information.

Relevance: Information should be directed toward the appropriate personnel. And only that information which aids those people in doing their jobs should reach them, to avoid an overload of extraneous information.

INTRANET

Intranets are subsets of the Internet, created by individual firms or organizations that wish to limit access to the information they contain or provide to only those authorized users to whom they specifically grant access.

- In other words, an intranet is a private network which utilizes all the technological advances the Internet employs, but secures its contents within specified boundaries
- These boundaries are established by the use of hardware and software firewalls, which permit access to only authorized users

EXTRANET

Extranets are also subsets of the Internet, in which a firm chooses to permit access to one or more of its intranets to a selected group of outside firms or individuals.

- In other words, an extranet is a semiprivate network using the public technologies of the Internet, combined with the firewall technologies of an intranet to enable selected business partners and customers to gain access to the common data which will assist the firm in pursuing its business objectives

INTERNET

The Internet is a vast global system of computer networks, interconnecting millions of computers in over 100 countries; in other words, the Internet is a network of networks, consisting of a vast array of government, private, academic, and business networks that are linked by a wide variety of optical and electronic technologies.

- The Internet contains an enormous quantity of information, most commonly encountered in interlinked documents using the computer language of hypertext to display their contents and in electronic-mail (e-mail) processing technology enabling users to communicate with one another
- The Internet has no central governing body but rather is governed by the individual networks which constitute it, each of which sets its own standards
- The Internet has become so omnipresent as to have permeated virtually all aspects of modern human life

INTEGRATED CIRCUIT IN A COMPUTER SYSTEM

An integrated circuit is a miniaturized electronic circuit that has been etched onto the surface of a silicon wafer known as a computer chip.

- Integrated circuits are now an essential component of virtually all electronic consumer products and electronic business devices
- By the mid-20th century, technological advances led to the development of the computer chip as a replacement for the old vacuum tubes, integrating large numbers of tiny transistors onto silicon wafers
- Computer chips have undergone steady advances in size, whereby ever-smaller chips are capable of holding an ever-greater number of electronic circuits

- The result is that the electrons need to travel much shorter distances, thus increasing the speed of transmission
- Nowadays, a single computer chip can contain literally millions of tiny circuits
- In fact, a chip the size of a thumbnail can now contain as much as a mile of electronic circuits

BROADBAND TECHNOLOGY

Broadband technology is a newer Internet technology which enables users to send and receive information at a vastly greater rate than the traditional dial-up technology.

- Dial-up technology utilizes standard phone lines to connect to the Internet via a modem, and limits the speed with which information is transmitted to a relatively tiny 56 kilobits per second
- By contrast, broadband handles a much wider range of frequencies, enabling multiple pieces of information, often divided into different channels (or frequency bins), to be transmitted simultaneously, resulting in a significantly faster transmission speed, often up to 50 times the speed of dial-up connections

SOFTWARE PROGRAMS

The tasks for which the following types of software programs are designed:

- *Word processing programs*: These programs are used in the creation, editing, and printing of documents. These are the most common types of programs in use today. The advantage that word processing programs have over a typewriter is their ability to massively edit a document without creating an entirely new one
- *Desktop publishing software*: These programs enable the user to combine text and graphics in a way that in the past could be created with only complex layout and design programs
- *Spreadsheet programs*: These programs create tables consisting of multiple rows and columns, enabling users to enter data which can be manipulated by mathematical functions
- *Database programs*: These are software applications that enable users to manipulate data in fields, records, and files that would ordinarily be contained in lists

COMPUTER EVOLUTIONARY PROCESS

Mainframe computers were first developed in the 1950s and dominated large computing systems through the 1990s.

- Massive boxes often filling huge rooms in a business operation, these mainframe computers were programmed by employees working at what were called "dumb" terminals, essentially keyboards and monitors with no independent computing ability
- Then in the 1990s, with the proliferation of personal computers and networked computer systems came the advent of client/server computing, in which these same employees had their own personal computer on their desks, linked directly to the network
- Here, a company's data are stored on a central computer known as a server and are uploaded upon request to an employee's own computer over the network connecting all the computers in the organization

IT ADVANCEMENT CHALLENGES

Perhaps the most significant opportunity presented by advances in IT is that presented by the Internet, enabling workers to telecommute rather than having to physically go to the work environment every day.

- By linking employees' computers to the company's network over the Internet, employees can transmit their work to the company and obtain the electronic resources necessary to do their jobs from the comfort of their homes
- Thus, travel time is reduced, productivity is potentially increased, and less financial resources are expended on office space
- Among the challenges IT presents, one is that firms must hire employees who are sufficiently technically sophisticated to operate the new systems
- Another challenge is that telecommuting can lead to a sense of distance or isolation, where telecommuting employees feel out of the office loop

GRAPHIC PROGRAMS

Graphics programs are a software program which is capable of generating images, ranging from elementary to highly complex, such as pie charts and graphs. Video clips, animation, and sound clips can also be added.

COMMUNICATIONS PROGRAMS

Communications programs are software programs that allow computers to exchange information with one another. Any data that a computer can create can be transmitted by communications programs, from text to graphic images and electronic mail.

MESSAGE CENTER SOFTWARE

Message center software is a comprehensive communication software packages that manage a whole range of communication methods, including voice mail, fax, and phone.

ACCOUNTING AND FINANCE PROGRAMS

Accounting and finance programs assist users in organizing financial date and generating financial reports; enables users to test out scenarios by entering one set of data, checking the results, and then repeating the task with alternate sets of data for comparison.

COMPUTER NETWORKS PRIVACY THREATS

E-mail is the prime vehicle by which criminals target individuals in order to steal their personal information.

- This personal information can then be used by the criminal to impersonate the victim, resulting in financial loss and emotional distress
- Typically, criminals send out e-mails en masse, which include various enticements to get the recipient to submit personal information such as Social Security numbers, birth dates, mothers' maiden names, etc.
- E-mails travel over the Internet and can be intercepted by hackers with a desire to read your messages
- Users of the Internet leave a trail of the sites they have visited, information that hackers can share without the user's knowledge or permission with others
- Companies and individuals can use this information to specifically target advertising or other less savory material to selected users

Major IT Security Challenges

A major issue faced by all firms utilizing computer networks is the attempt to steal the firms' computer data.

- In recent years, over 40 percent of US companies have reported attempts to break into their computer systems
- Data are stolen by hackers seeking to disrupt computer systems, by employees who steal information for personal gain, or by competitors seeking to attain a competitive advantage or are merely lost due to incompetence or poor system design
- Data loss is even experienced by the government, with hackers having broken into the Pentagon's systems as well as those of other government agencies
- Computer viruses are pieces of malignant software which are placed by unscrupulous persons on the Internet or directly onto organizations' computer systems
- There, the virus proliferates, incapacitating or debilitating the host systems and spreading its effects throughout all other computers on the network
- Finally, the practice of phishing occurs when unscrupulous persons attempt to entice users to reveal personal information, which can then be used for financial gain

Psychologist Abraham Maslow's

Psychologist Abraham Maslow sought to understand what motivates employees at work, and he concluded that they were motivated by a series of needs which could be identified and enumerated. He felt that these needs could be arranged in a hierarchy of increasingly rewarding levels. His idea was that as one need was fulfilled, the worker would move on to the next higher need in the hierarchy. Here is Maslow's hierarchy of needs:

- Physiological needs: food, shelter, etc.
- Safety needs: the need to feel free from danger
- Social needs: the need to be considered a valued associate
- Esteem needs: the need for self-respect and recognition from others
- Self-actualization needs: the need to express one's potential

Intrinsic Reward

Intrinsic reward is the personal satisfaction an employee or worker obtains after performance of an assignment thoroughly and well.

Extrinsic Reward

Extrinsic reward is something of value an employee or worker is given by superiors as an expression of their appreciation for a job well done. Examples: praise, recognition, bonuses, salary increases.

Scientific Management

Scientific management is the discipline developed by Frederick Taylor in which management seeks to learn the most effective ways for employees to perform their work.

Time-Motion Studies

A time-motion study is another discipline developed by Frederick Taylor, in which jobs are broken down into tasks and the time required to complete these tasks.

Principle of Motion Economy

Principle of motion economy is a theory which asserts that work can be broken down into a series of elementary motions

Job Enrichment

Job enrichment is a theory which postulates that the nature of the actual work is the most important and effective area by which to motivate employees. Give employees an identifiable task which they are to perform through to its completion, the theory asserts, and the employees will naturally want to carry this task out. The five characteristics of work which advocates of job enrichment feel must be addressed are:

- Skill variety: a measure of the variety of skills a job requires
- Task identity: a measure of to what extent a task has a recognizable completion point
- Task significance: a measure of how much impact the job has on other employees
- Autonomy: a measure of the degree of independence in a particular job
- Feedback: a measure of the amount of information that individual workers get regarding their job performance

Frederick Herzberg

Psychologist Frederick Herzberg sought to discern what job-related factors were most influential in motivating employees to do their best. He came up with a rather long list of factors which he deemed the most important. He further observed that these factors could be broken up into distinct groups:

- One group involved considerations that were more or less centered upon job content, such as a sense of achievement and recognition, he termed these group motivators
- The other group centered more upon the job environment, such as working conditions, salary, and job security
- Perhaps surprisingly, Herzberg concluded that it was the first group which provided the strongest motivation for workers. In other words, he felt that considerations like salary, which most people assume are of prime importance, are superseded by considerations of self-esteem in the workplace

Goal Setting Theory

This theory asserts that management can effectively provide motivation to employees by setting ambitious but attainable goals. Further, employees respond to feedback on their job performance. Finally, each department and individual should be involved in setting goals and meeting them.

Management by Objectives

This theory is based on the idea that management must create the proper environment for workers and that only by doing this will workers be sufficiently self-motivated to accomplish the company's objectives. That is, management does not motivate people; people motivate themselves given the right circumstances.

Expectancy Theory

This theory posits that employees' motivation to accomplish a specific task is directly dependent upon their expectations regarding the outcome of that task. That is, employees ask themselves:

- Can I accomplish the task?
- What is my reward if I accomplish it?
- Is the reward worth the effort?

McGregor's Theory X and Theory Y

McGregor's management Theory X and Theory Y are different ways to assess what it is that motivates employees. Theory X and Theory Y contain diametrically opposed and contradictory points of view, as follows:

- Theory X concludes that average employees are motivated primarily by the desire for money and that they dislike work and can be sufficiently motivated to do their jobs only through control and threats
- It further concludes that employees actually wish to be treated in this manner
- By contrast, Theory Y rests on the assumptions that employees enjoy work and are naturally motivated to want to do a good job
- Further, it asserts that employees welcome responsibility and are capable of high degrees of imagination
- Theory Y postulates that employees should be given the responsibility to design solutions to their work-related issues and that management should get out of their way and let them do their job

Manager's Challenges

As business moves to a more global setting, increasing cultural and ethnic diversity in the workplace indicates that managers will not be able to apply a one-size-fits-all strategy to motivate employees.

- Managers will more and more have to become personally involved with and informed about their workers' needs and backgrounds
- Cultural differences are not necessarily limited to ethnic or geographical origins
- The workplace now contains and in the future will continue to contain employees with wide age differentials and, consequently, the different cultural values associated with each of their generational identities. For example, older workers from the Baby Boom generation have significantly different backgrounds and life experiences from Gen X'ers and Gen Y'ers
- Certain motivators go beyond cultural, ethnic, or age differentials, however
- By acknowledging and rewarding in an appropriate manner a job well done, managers are likely in most circumstances to be rewarded with employees eager to do their best work

Reinforcement Theory

Reinforcement theory states that both positive and negative feedback provide motivations for people to act in certain ways. In other words, reinforcement theory may be defined as the proverbial carrot-and-stick approach, whereby both rewards (such as praise or recognition) and punishments (such as reprimands or financial penalties) are utilized to obtain the desired result.

Equity Theory

Equity theory concerns itself with these questions an employee asks:

- If I succeed at my job, will it have been worth the effort?
- What is fair?
- These questions are asked in the context of a comparison with other employees performing similar tasks
- In other words: If I succeed, will I be compensated in a similar manner as another employee who succeeds?
- All other circumstances being comparable, am I being treated in roughly the same manner as other employees?

Firm's Human Resources

Create an inventory of the firm's employees: In addition to demographic information such as age and educational level, identify such information as different skill levels and languages spoken, etc.

Create job analyses: Identify what work is performed by which employees, including job title, job description, and job specifications (i.e., the specific skills required for the job).

Estimate future personnel requirements: Plan ahead to anticipate future requirements.

Estimate future supply: Analyze the workforce to determine the future availability of employees with specific skills.

Develop a strategic plan: Address such issues as recruiting, employee selection, training, salary requirements, and scheduling.

Human Resources Challenges

Human resource challenges that are faced today are:

- Shortages of highly trained workers
- Large numbers of workers whose skills need upgrading
- A growing number of poorly educated workers
- The proliferation of new laws promoting social consciousness
- More and more single-parent families
- Continued downsizing
- Competition from overseas labor
- A highly age-diverse population
- Increased demand for tailored benefits
- Growing concern over health care and elder care
- Reduced employee loyalty

Employee's Selection Process

Obtain complete applications: Job applications are now much more complex than in the past, when they were limited to questions about past employment and skill and educational levels.

Conduct interviews: Once a one- or two-step process, interviews are now much more in-depth, often conducted initially through an outside recruiter and then by an initial staff member, his manager, and finally the department manager.

Conduct tests: Skill tests are used more and more these days to weed out applicants without the necessary skills for the job.

Do background investigations: In addition to checks of criminal records, these investigations may include credit history and school records.

Do physical exams: Now more prevalent than ever, such investigations may include drug tests and mental health screenings.

Allow for probationary periods: Here, a new hire must demonstrate the ability to do the job and to adequately fit into the corporate culture.

HR Recruiting Difficulties

It is occasionally the case that it is difficult to find prospective employees with the skills and training required to perform the job in question.

- This is an especially difficult problem for smaller businesses
- One solution is to hire employees who in other respects fit well into the firm's corporate culture but who will need to be trained on the job
- Just because a prospective employee has the necessary technical and educational skills to perform the job does not guarantee a good fit within the organization
- Because companies have their own cultural identities, it is important to select employees who will fit well into the firm's established culture
- Many organizations are subject to an array of union rules, government regulations, and other such constraints, thus limiting the pool of potential new hires
- Finally, job mobility has been on the increase for years
- Employees frequently have their ear to the ground in order to take advantage of outside opportunities offering better salary compensation or more desirable working conditions

Job Training

The following types of job training:

- *Employee orientation*: New employees are introduced to the organization and its policies and procedures
- *On-the-job training*: New employees learn their jobs by watching others or by beginning to perform them themselves
- *Apprentice programs*: New employees learn their jobs under the mentorship of experienced employees
- Off-the-job training: Training occurs off the worksite, including at classes or seminars
- *Online training*: Classes or courses are conducted held on the Internet, where employees can learn on their own time
- *Vestibule training*: Employees receive training near the worksite, using equipment similar to that which they will use on the job
- *Job simulation*: Like the training that pilots receive, employees learn on equipment that duplicates that which they use work at the work site

Contract, Contingent, and Part-Time Workers

Hiring full-time employees is a major commitment made by a firm. For one thing, the firm often has to pay benefits and offer some guarantee of continued employment or compensation in the case of termination or layoff; plus, it can be difficult to remove an unsatisfactory employee.

Hiring contract, part-time, and contingency workers is one practical solution.

- In addition to providing firms with the flexibility to respond to ever-changing market demands, these workers are often highly specialized and capable of coming in at short notice with all the necessary skills to do the immediate job at hand
- The firm is not responsible for paying the extensive benefits often offered to full-time employees
- For many workers, this type of work fits well into their mobile and varied lifestyle
- Such work offers them opportunities to pursue more personal interests and doesn't require the kind of commitment that often comes with a full-time position

Performance Appraisal

Establish performance standards: Guideposts that have been accepted by management which define reasonable and attainable standards to judge worker performance.

Communicate these standards: Employees cannot be expected to intuitively know these standards and must be provided with them.

Evaluate performance: This involves comparing the employee's performance against the standards set out and communicated, as above. Results. Managers and employees engage in a dialogue in which successes and areas in need of improvement are identified.

Take corrective action: Managers offer constructive feedback to assist employees in improving their performance.

Use the results to make decisions: Promotions, pay increases, and the need for additional training are based upon the appraisals outlined above.

Management Training Programs

On-the-job coaching: This occurs when personnel from senior management mentor lower-level managers, teaching them needed skills and providing direction and feedback.

Understudy positions: This type of training consists of assigning junior managers to work as assistants to higher-level managers, assisting them in the performance of their duties.

Job rotation: This is the practice of assigning managers varied, revolving positions within the organization, in order to familiarize them with the variety of tasks the organization requires.

Off-the-job courses and seminars: In order to advance their technical and interpersonal skills, managers are periodically sent to classes or seminars held at outside schools or universities to learn new skills.

Pay Systems

Salary: Employees receive a fixed amount, computed weekly, biweekly, or monthly. Employees receive no extra pay for overtime.

Hourly wage: Compensation is computed on the number of hours or days worked. Typically, these employees do receive overtime pay but receive no benefits, such as health insurance.

Piecework: Pay is based on the number of units or items produced.

Commission: Pay is calculated as a percentage of sales.

Bonus plans: Employees receive extra pay or other benefits for meeting or exceeding certain stated objectives.

Profit sharing: Employees receive annual bonuses, computed as some percentage of the firm's profits.

Stock options: Employees receive the right to purchase the firm's stock at a specific price.

Firm Benefits

First and foremost, attractive and competitive compensation and benefits packages attract the kinds of personnel the firm will value, and in sufficient quantities.

- These packages are likely to inspire employees to work productively
- Further, attractive compensation and benefits tend to inspire employee loyalty, providing the firm with a steady workforce which is less likely to jump to other firms
- A well-managed compensation and benefits program helps a firm remain competitive through achieving low costs as a result of their employees' job satisfaction and its concomitant high productivity
- Finally, employees who are well compensated are likely to gain a sense of their own financial security, which should be a goal of any enlightened firm

Flextime Plans

Flextime plans are attractive alternatives to the proverbial nine-to-five (or longer, especially in high-tech occupations) schedule of the past.

- Flextime plans allow employees a degree of freedom to choose their start and end times, such as 6 a.m. to 2 p.m. or 10 a.m. to 6 p.m.
- A great advantage for many employees is that flextime offers them a way to beat the crush of rush-hour traffic
- A compressed workweek is another option, in which an employee works his full complement of 40 hours per week, but instead of spreading those hours over five 8-hour days, the employee may work, say, four 10-hour days, thus giving him a three-day weekend
- Telecommuting is another possibility, enabling workers to work from home, thus saving on driving time and expense and allowing them to put in their required hours any time of the day that is convenient for them

Fringe Benefits

In a world in which unemployment is high and jobs scarce, firms must make an effort to attract the best employees. Offering fringe benefits is one way to do this.

- In fact, recently fringe benefits have grown faster than wages, accounting for as much as 30 percent of payrolls
- Many employees are now requesting fringe benefits instead of salary, as this way they can avoid paying higher taxes on their earnings
- Fringe benefits come in many different forms—for example, sick-leave pay, vacation pay, pension plans, and health plans
- Fringe benefits can even include club memberships or discounts, home-mortgage assistance, day-care services, and the use of company cars
- The term cafeteria-style benefits refer to the practice of allowing employees to choose from a menu of fringe benefit options, up to a specified dollar amount

Civil Rights Acts of 1964 and 1991 Effect on HR

The Civil Rights Act of 1964 was one of the most important and far-reaching pieces of social legislation in the history of the United States.

- The intent of the legislation was to eliminate discrimination based upon race, religion, sex, or national origin in hiring, firing, compensation, and a broad array of other aspects of employment
- Thus, its impact has been profound and has affected virtually all aspects of the operations of human resource management
- The act was later amended to include age as another condition which could not be used as a basis for discrimination
- And in 1972, the Equal Employment Opportunity Act (EEOA) was added as an amendment
- EEOA strengthened the Equal Employment Opportunity Commission, giving it the ability to enforce the mandates of the EEOA
- The Civil Rights Act of 1972 further strengthened antidiscrimination efforts, enabling victims of discrimination to pursue their cases in jury trials and to be awarded compensatory and punitive damages if such discrimination is proved

Employee Exit Reasons

Employees who have fulfilled and exceeded the requirements of their jobs may be promoted to higher positions.

- Or they may be reassigned to another area of the firm, in order to gain broader experience or to make up for a personnel shortage in the new area
- Employees may also be terminated for a variety of reasons, among them unacceptable job performance, personality clashes, or conduct detrimental to the firm
- However, except in cases where it is unavoidable, such as economic imperatives, termination is rarely a desirable option, as there are now an array of potential legal consequences an employer may incur at the hands of a terminated employee
- Employees may be offered early retirement packages as an enticement to leave a firm, rather than being terminated, given the potential legal consequences the firm might face
- Finally, valued employees may leave a firm because they have a better offer elsewhere
- Firms need to be aware of their relative position in the marketplace, in order to ensure that their compensation packages are competitive.

Labor Unions

Labor unions are an employee organization whose principal objective is to represent their members in negotiations with management over worker-related issues such as financial compensation, working conditions, and benefits packages.

- Unions originally sought to protect workers from unsafe or otherwise intolerable working conditions, as well as to gain some measure of participation in the decision-making processes of management
- Unions have thus sought to obtain for their members what they consider to be a reasonable share of the profits generated by their efforts

Legislative Protects Disabled and Older Employees

Earlier legislative efforts focused on addressing issues of discrimination specifically as they related to race and sex.

- In 1973, the Vocational Rehabilitation Act offered similar protections for people with physical or mental disabilities
- The Americans with Disabilities Act of 1990 enhanced these protections, requiring firms to make "reasonable accommodations" for employees with disabilities, such as modifications to equipment like headsets and physical access structures like ramps
- The Age Discrimination in Employment Act of 1967 was put forward specifically to protect workers over the age of 40 from employment discrimination based upon their age
- Affecting only firms with 20 or more employees, the act also protects older workers from being forced into mandatory retirement, except in cases where it has been shown that being over a certain age might pose a danger to the public, as in the case of airline pilots

Historical Labor Organizations

Knights of Labor: the first truly national labor organization in the United States, the stated mission of the Knights of Labor was to attain political power, and in so doing transform the US economy. Formed in 1869, the Knights were open to both labor and management and promoted social causes in addition to economic issues.

American Federation of Labor (AFL): a rival to the Knights of Labor, the AFL focused its efforts on bettering the working conditions for what were termed craftspeople, i.e., skilled workers who the AFL felt would be better able to command sufficient bargaining power to influence management.

Congress of Industrial Organizations (CIO): formed in response to the AFL's exclusion of unskilled workers and attempted to bring together both types of workers in order to enhance labor's influence. The CIO soon had as many members as its rival, the AFL, and finally in 1955 the two organizations merged into the AFL-CIO.

Labor Unions Criticisms

Labor unions have been criticized for working for the benefit of their members to the detriment of non-union workers, consumers of the products sold by their parent firms, and shareholders in the firms in which the unions are present.

- Unions have been accused of harming the general public by engaging in strikes which have led to disruptions in crucial public services such as transportation and health care
- Some firms have leveled the charge that unions tend to unfairly drive up wages to the point where the resulting diminution of profits generated by the firm make it unable to compete on a level playing field with its competitors
- Management has also complained that unions' bargaining power vastly increases a firm's operating expenses, as a result of the increasingly expensive legal services having to be performed

Agreements Reached in Negotiations

Negotiated labor-management agreement: Commonly referred to as a labor contract, a negotiated labor-management agreement defines the terms and conditions under which labor and management will interact.

Closed shop agreement: This union-generated restriction, outlawed by the 1947 Labor-Management Relations Act, said that workers seeking employment with a firm had to become union members.

Union shop agreement: Here, workers are not required to be union members to be hired but must join the union within a specified period of time.

Agency agreement: This permits employers to hire non-union workers who are not required to join the union but nevertheless must pay some form of dues or fees.

Open shop agreement: This agreement gives workers the option to either join or not join a union.

HR and Union Concepts

Yellow-dog contract: a device utilized by management to combat union organizing, whereby employees seeking to be hired are required to agree not to join a union

Collective bargaining: a process pursued and strongly supported by the AFL, in which unions and management meet to negotiate such concerns as wages and hours, the result of which is a legally binding contract expressing the results of such negotiations

Certification: the process by which a union attains official recognition by the National Labor Relations Board, whose duty is to oversee relations between labor and management

Decertification: designed to free workers from the obligation to be union members, a process whereby workers disavow a union as its workplace representative

Labor Strikes

A strike, also referred to a strike action, is the process whereby a labor union or other organized group of workers refuses to go to work en masse in an attempt to force management to relieve worker grievances.

- Strikes came into prominent use during the Industrial Revolution, as factories and mines began to employ mass labor
- Initially, most countries made it illegal for workers to strike, and it has only been in the last 200 years that strikes have been made at least partially legal, at least in Western countries
- Among the activities carried out by workers during a strike are, in addition to work stoppage, picketing the company and using media such as newspapers, TV, and the Internet to publicize their cause
- Strikes can be particularly effective in garnering public support—if not for the strikers themselves, then for a general resolution to the conflict—in cases where public services are affected, causing considerable inconvenience to the public at large

Grievance

A grievance may be defined as a claim brought by employees asserting that management is failing to honor the terms arrived at in the negotiated labor-management agreement, typically concerning issues such as overtime, promotions, transfers, and layoffs.

Mediation

In mediation, labor and management turn to a third party known as a mediator, whose role is to encourage the two parties to continue to negotiate and to offer -impartial—that is, in the interests of neither labor nor management—recommendations to resolve the conflict. Importantly, mediators do not have the power to make decisions, only to make suggestions.

ARBITRATION

Arbitration is similar to mediation, in that a third party is brought in to facilitate resolution of a labor dispute. Under arbitration, however, the arbitrator renders a decision to which both sides must agree and to which they are legally bound.

UNION MOVEMENT

Recent and rapidly developing changes in global business have had a profound effect on the union movement.

- Union membership has declined significantly in recent years
- And global competition, outsourcing, and the increasingly technological nature of work have forced unions to relinquish many of the gains they had achieved over 200 years
- Unions have naturally resisted such developments but have had to make significant wage and benefit concessions in order to keep jobs
- Recognizing the difficulties presented by current events, unions have in recent years made efforts to team up with management in such practices as the training of workers, even going so far as to assist management in the process of helping to recruit and train foreign workers
- In these efforts to make labor-management relations less confrontational, both unions and management can hope to better work together in their mutual interest

MANAGEMENT TACTICS

A lockout is one of the tactics employed by management in response to a strike.

- A lockout may be described as a kind of reverse strike, in which management closes the workplace in an attempt to put pressure on the strikers to abandon their cause
- The theory is that by denying workers their wages, these workers will soon abandon their efforts and return to work
- Management has also sought injunctions to force striking employees back on the job
- An injunction is a court order directing a party to perform (or to refrain from performing) certain specified acts, under penalty of civil or criminal action
- In the case of a strike, the injunction sought by management would compel workers to return to work
- Management may also hire strikebreakers, derogatorily termed scabs, to perform the work that the regular workers have abandoned, a practice much loathed by the strikers themselves

PAY EQUITY CONCEPT

As more and more women have entered the workforce, issues of financial compensation have become a more visible challenge to management.

- Pay equity refers to the difference in earnings between men and women performing essentially the same job
- It is true that there have been advances in women attaining a more equitable share of salary benefits—in 1963, when the Equal Pay Act was passed, women earned on average $.59 for every dollar a man earned, whereas in 2008 their paychecks reflected earnings of $.78 for every dollar a man in a comparable job earned
- As recently as the 1980s, the concept of comparable worth emerged, which argued that people in jobs requiring roughly similar levels of education, training, and experience should receive roughly similar levels of financial compensation

- However, government and especially management rejected the idea, claiming that it would not necessarily lead to more equilibrium in the workforce
- This issue promises to continue to be a challenge in the years ahead

Executive Compensation

Executive compensation has been a hot topic in the news lately, as upper management and especially CEOs in major firms have reaped colossal financial rewards while the companies they run have taken huge losses, resulting in many of them having to accept large government bailouts in the form of taxpayer dollars to avoid their failure causing a devastating ripple effect throughout the economy as a whole.

- Several decades ago, top executives could expect to earn significantly more than line employees, but recently that gap has expanded dramatically, to the extent that some CEOs have earned enough in one year to equal what an ordinary employee would have to work for tens of thousands of years to equal
- Predictably, the public reaction has been one of dismay and rage
- Their main complaint is that these CEOs' enormous pay and benefits packages seem totally unrelated to the firms' performance
- Unions have been particularly vocal in their opposition to outsized executive compensation

Sexual Harassment

Sexual harassment refers to unwelcome sexual advances, in the form of bullying, coercion, or the promise of rewards in exchange for sexual favors. Sexual harassment in the workplace contributes to a hostile work environment, and in certain circumstances is illegal.

Workplace Violence

Violence in the workplace is a growing area of concern, with OSHA (the Occupational Safety and Health Administration) reporting that homicide in the workplace is responsible for 16 percent of all workplace deaths.

- The expression "going postal" arose from the 1986 tragedy in which a postal employee killed 14 fellow workers before committing suicide
- Sexual harassment was one of the topics addressed in the 1991 Civil Rights Act, and in 1996 the Supreme Court expanded the definition of what may be considered a hostile work environment to include unwelcome behavior such as sexual harassment
- Firms have taken preventative action to address violence in the workplace, including focus groups and forums for employees to express their considerations

Child Care and Elder Care

Child care has become an increasingly important issue to be addressed by management, especially since the recent influx of women into the workplace.

- Absences related to child care issues are reported to cost American businesses billions of dollars every year
- Companies have attempted to assist employees with child care concerns by offering discounts with child care chains, vouchers, on-site day care centers, and access to referral services which can recommend high-quality child care facilities

The number of people over age 65 is expected to double to 77 million by the year 2040.

- This aging of the US population has led to increased concern over the issue of elder care
- Some of the measures companies have taken to address this issue include offering flextime, telecommuting, employee assistance programs, and even health spending accounts in which employees can put pre-tax income for elder care expenses

Contemporary Issues

Transactional Site

Transactional site: This is the type of website most familiar to people who shop online. A transactional site can be an electronic storefront for a traditional brick-and-mortar business establishment, or it can be the Internet-based selling tool of a catalog operation. Typically these sites allow for complete transactions, where customers place their orders, pay for them, and receive support after the sale.

Information Delivery Site

Information delivery site: Sites of this variety, unlike transactional sites, do not sell products online. By contrast, information delivery sites function in a manner similar to brochures, where the goal is to provide corporate awareness rather than sales.

E-Marketplaces

E-marketplaces: These sites bring buyers and sellers together and in the process receive a percentage of the sale amount. The most recognized e-marketplace is eBay.

E-Commerce

These four types of e-commerce:

- B2B: Business to business refers to the practice of businesses selling their goods and services to other businesses—for example, manufacturers selling to distributors, or wholesalers selling to retailers
- B2C: Business to consumer is where businesses sell to the general public through their websites, typically using shopping cart software
- C2B: Consumer to business is the process whereby a consumer proposes a project that she is interested in selling or developing, in the hope that businesses will bid on the project
- C2C: Consumer to consumer e-commerce takes place through websites offering free classified ads, auctions, and other forums for individuals to buy and sell products using online payment services such as PayPal

Static Website

A static website is one in which the pages that reside on the Web server are the same as the websites which consumers view on the World Wide Web. That is, they display predefined, unmodifiable images to consumers, allowing them no significant way in which to interact with the site. These sites may be referred to as informational, in that they resemble brochures designed to present consistent, standard information.

Dynamic Website

By contrast, dynamic websites are those that change frequently or that interacts with the user based on the results of a search or other request. Dynamic websites may be conceptualized as individual, customized sites which tailor their appearance and attributes to the user. Other terms for a dynamic website are "dynamic HTML" and "dynamic content."

Website

A website is a collection of related and interlinked electronic "pages" on the Internet which contain a combination of text, graphics, and sound and animated elements. Some websites are public—in other words, visible to anyone who desires to visit them; or they can be by subscription access only, i.e., to get beyond the home page to the more detailed content of the site, the consumer must subscribe, often by paying a monthly fee.

A website can be a personal website, a commercial website, a government website, or a nonprofit website such as an educational website. The collection of all publicly accessible websites constitutes what is known as the World Wide Web.

The software which defines the characteristics of a website is designed and programmed by a web developer and resides on a special computer called a Web server.

Internet Taxation

Currently, an individual or organization that makes an online purchase pays no sales taxes. Clearly, though, there is a great deal of money involved in Internet sales, due to the immense volume of these transactions.

- Government, naturally, has taken great interest in this issue. State and local policymakers have pushed for a piece of these profits and have been assiduously attempting to change the tax code to enable them to do this. Advocates of taxing Internet transactions make the claim that the tax-exempt status of e-commerce transactions is in essence a form of tax evasion on a grand scale.
- Opponents of taxing Internet transactions make the case that to impose taxes would stifle the growth of Internet business. They further assert that any attempt to tax the internet would be a minefield of conflicting interests, where competition among jurisdictions would be too complex to implement. They further assert that consumers would simply make fewer purchases over the Internet if this advantage were taken away.

Internet Regulation

The global, borderless nature of the Internet has raised questions about how it can be regulated to implement national interests.

- One reason to seek such regulation is that the Internet provides irresponsible persons or criminal entities the opportunity to prey on consumers by engaging in fraudulent activities or committing identity theft
- The Federal Trade Commission has been actively involved in efforts to work with other countries in the interest of enforcing international consumer protection laws
- The FTC has not gone so far as to advocate the formation of a particular oversight body to enforce such regulations; rather, it seeks ways to persuade private industry and governments to work together to promote internationally acceptable standards of fair practices

Website Design Components

Domain name: Domain name simply is the name that identifies a website. For example:

- AOL.com identifies America on Line
- Good search engine optimization (SEO) begins with a good name

Text information: Text information are the words that appear directly on the site. Ideally, these words, in addition to conveying information to the viewer of the site, should contain keywords which exploit SEO.

Navigation components: Navigation components are those elements that make it easy and intuitive to move from one part of the site to another, through the effective use of menus and drop-down boxes.

Links: Links are click-on connections from a website to other, related websites. In turn, good links to the website from other websites increase traffic.

SEO: Search engine optimization (SEO) is the art and science of making websites attractive to search engines such as Google and Yahoo.

- SEO is a process by which the owner of a website attempts to include in the design of the site certain triggers which will result in a greater volume of traffic to the website
- Properly utilizing SEO will result in a website receiving a high ranking by search engines such as Google and Yahoo
- When this happens, the site will appear near the top of their lists, resulting in more traffic to the site
- Note that SEO may make it look like the website designer is optimizing or making changes to a search engine like Google, but this is not the case. In actuality, the designer is optimizing the website, so that when someone types specific search terms into a search engine, the website in question appears near the top of Google's list of relevant sites

Ethics and Legality

In the early 2000s, a series of ethical scandals at Enron, WorldCom, Tyco International, and other corporations, both large and small, led to a serious examination of the issue of ethics in business.

- Ethics in business addresses such issues as fiduciary responsibility, corporate governance, insider trading, bribery, and accounting irregularities
- It is noteworthy that some of these scandals involved behavior which many considered to be wildly inappropriate and ethically repugnant, although no actual laws were broken—hence the distinction between unethical conduct and illegal conduct, where actual laws have been broken
- Of course, no one would disagree with the contention that those individuals who actually did break the law should be punished as the law permits
- But laws in and of themselves are not sufficient to induce people to behave more honestly
- For this reason, it is incumbent upon business organizations to establish clear standards for ethical conduct and to educate their workforces to be familiar with and to strive to uphold these standards

Passwords

Passwords are used in conjunction with user IDs (names that computer users assign to themselves) to help users remain anonymous to unauthorized individuals or businesses. Passwords range in strength from weak to very strong, depending on how complex they are. For example, passwords such as pet names or birthdays are considered weak, whereas passwords consisting of seemingly random characters, utilizing both upper- and lowercase letters and numbers, are considered stronger.

Encryption

Encryption is the conversion of data from one form to another, typically one that is difficult for unauthorized people or organizations to understand. In encryption, the data are passed through a scrambling algorithm, the resulting output being unrecognizable as a human language. In order to decipher the encrypted output—that is, to convert it back into its original, comprehensible form—the user at the other end utilizes another algorithm that undoes the work of the scrambling algorithm.

Compliance-Based Ethics

Compliance-based ethics is a method of preventing unlawful or unethical behavior through the use of control and the institution of punishments for violations. One complaint against compliance-based ethics is that any behavior which is not specifically defined may be considered legal just because it fell through the cracks.

Integrity-Based Ethics Codes

Integrity-based ethics codes is whereby the organization emphasizes personal responsibility to create an environment in which workers think for themselves, employing their innate sense of right and wrong.

Whistleblower

Whistleblower is a person who reports unethical or illegal conduct. New regulations protect whistleblowers from retaliation by those individuals or organizations whose behavior they report.

Cheating and Unethical Conduct

Recent studies have discovered a direct correlation between academic dishonesty among undergraduate students and unethical behavior among these same students when they enter the workforce.

- The most prevalent form of academic dishonesty is plagiarism, in which a student copies verbatim material found on a given subject written by someone else, typically these days material found on the Internet
- The advent of word processing software and cut-and-paste technology has enabled students and others to directly insert the work of others into their own
- In response to instances of academic dishonesty, many educational institutions have begun to use services like TurnItIn.com, which detect plagiarism in seconds. Also, many of these institutions have adopted severe penalties for such unethical conduct

CSR

Corporate social responsibility (CSR) may be defined as the proposition that businesses should not focus exclusively on bottom-line profits but should make an effort to contribute to the welfare of society as a whole. Some ways in which firms can demonstrate corporate social responsibility are:

- Corporate philanthropy, such as gifts to nonprofit organizations serving societal interests such as education, the arts, and health
- Corporate social initiatives, similar to corporate philanthropy, except that corporate social initiatives utilize the firm's specific competencies for the general good, such as a pharmaceutical firm donating medicine or medical supplies to the needy
- Corporate responsibility, including such practices as equality in hiring, providing a safe work environment, and recycling
- Corporate policy, as it expresses the firm's positions on social and political issues

Improve America's Business Ethics

The six-step process by which firms can help to improve America's business ethics are the following:

1. Management must set out a clearly defined code of ethical conduct
2. Employees must be aware of the standards set in (1.) above, and must be made aware that they are expected to adhere to these standards
3. Managers and others must receive training to recognize the difference between acceptable and unethical behavior
4. Firms should establish an ethics office or department to respond to reports of unethical behavior
5. Outside business associates should be included in discussions about the firm's ethical principles and should be held responsible for their own noncompliance
6. The ethics defined above must be enforced with a mix of punishment and education

Firm's Considerations to Investors

Clearly, individuals and institutional investors who purchase a company's stock do so with the intention of making a profit. So, a firm's efforts toward bettering investor relations must be centered on making the firm successful in the marketplace.

- In addition to providing these investors with a good return on their investment, firms must also seek to avoid certain types of behavior which will cast their management in an unfavorable light to their stockholders
- One of these types of behaviors is the practice of backdating, whereby upper management receives part of their financial compensation in the form of stock options, yet is permitted to change the effective date of these stock option purchases to a point in time prior to the date they were granted in order to take advantage of a lower share price at the earlier date
- Another unethical type of behavior is insider trading, where certain individuals have exclusive knowledge of some future development at the company which will result in a steep rise in share value, thus having an unfair advantage over the general investing public

Firm's Commitment to Customers

It should be self-evident that if a firm intends to succeed, it must make an effort to be responsible to its customers.

- Narrowly defined, this responsibility includes offering them goods and services of high quality and at a reasonable and competitive price
- But this responsibility also includes such practices as providing excellent customer support, whereby customers can get their questions answered or their complaints addressed
- In the case of complaints about defective products, a good rule of thumb is: An ounce of prevention is worth a pound of cure
- If a firm responds slowly or inadequately to customer complaints, its reputation may suffer, resulting in an adverse effect on future sales

FIRM ACCRUES BENEFITS

Businesses that exercise responsibility to society and the environment naturally receive the goodwill of the communities in which they reside and in which they do business.

- In essence, exercising responsibility to society and the environment, in addition to serving the general good, provides a firm with outstanding promotion of its brand.
- Contributions to such enterprises as charitable institutions, arts foundations, and community-oriented volunteer efforts are common ways for a firm to pursue activities beneficial to society
- And exercising an appreciation for environmental issues can be a good business practice as well as one which is beneficial to society at large
- Particular value can be obtained when a firm located in a foreign country exercises social and environmental responsibility, as these types of activities can make the difference between a firms being resented as an outsider and being appreciated as a valued member of society

RESPONSIBILITY TO EMPLOYEES

The first way a firm can demonstrate responsibility to its employees is to provide jobs. Then, the firm must garner the goodwill of its employees by:

- Treating them in a respectful manner
- By providing satisfactory working conditions
- Including them in the decision-making process
- Being responsive to their grievances
- The firm can make great strides in demonstrating its sense of responsibility to its employees through its salary and benefits packages
- Not only do competitive wage and benefits packages increase worker satisfaction and sense of self-worth, but the result of such practices is that fewer employees leave the firm in search of better benefits elsewhere
- Another consideration is that the enlightened treatment of employees results in a safer workplace, so that disgruntled workers do not strike back at the firm

FREE TRADE

Free trade may be defined as the movement of goods and services among nations in the absence of hindrances such as protective customs tariffs, quotas, or other such political or economic barriers.

- Comparative advantage theory posits that countries should export to other countries those goods and services it most efficiently produces; the corollary being that countries should buy those products from other countries that can make them more efficiently
- By contrast, absolute advantage theory describes the situation whereby one country has the ability to produce a particular good or service at a lower cost per unit than any other country

SOCIAL AUDIT

A social audit consists of an evaluation of a firm's effectiveness in performing socially and environmentally responsible activities. A social audit is a process performed for the internal benefit of a firm, and is typically not made available to the public. The four main groups which monitor a firm's social responsibility are:

- Investors, who try to ensure that a firm extends its own socially conscious standards to its suppliers
- Environmentalists, who put pressure on firms which they feel are acting in environmentally irresponsible ways
- Union officials, whose goal is to identify instances in which a firm violates its stated policies or agreements
- Customers, who stop buying a firm's goods and services if they feel the firm is engaged in unethical behavior

BALANCE OF TRADE

Balance of trade refers to the difference in value between a country's total exports compared with its total imports over a specified span of time. If a country's exports are greater than its imports, it is said to have a favorable balance of trade.

TRADE DEFICIT

Trade deficit is when the value of a country's total imports exceeds the value of its total exports.

BALANCE OF PAYMENTS

Balance of payments is a systematic record of all economic transactions, including imports, exports, and such other factors as economic aid, tourism, and foreign investment. A country's goal is to have more money flowing into the country than is flowing out.

DUMPING

Dumping occurs when one country sells its goods in another country at a lower price than it charges its customers in its own domestic market.

FREE TRADE PROS AND CONS

Pros of free trade include:

- There are 6 billion potential customers worldwide
- Countries that have a comparative advantage producing certain goods and services will have growth in productivity
- Inexpensive imports keep costs down, thus mitigating the effects of inflation
- Protectionism in the form of tariffs is expensive
- Cooperation in one area may foster cooperation in others
- Free trade promotes economic growth

Cons of free trade include:

- Imports can cost domestic workers their jobs
- Lower labor costs in foreign countries may drive down wages elsewhere
- Free trade can lead to companies moving overseas to where the costs of production are less, thus costing jobs
- Free trade can lead a country to overspecialization through comparative advantage
- Exporting, and describe how exporting is beneficial as a strategy to compete in global markets

Exporting

Exporting is simply the process of a firm sending its products or services to foreign countries where they will be sold (or traded).

- The most obvious benefit derived from exporting is the potential to increase sales and raise the exporter's productivity
- Exporting leads to a firm expanding and increasing the size of its workforce
- Exporting offers a firm the opportunity to diversify its customer base, thus reducing its dependence upon a narrow market
- Exporting can lengthen a product's life cycle, by introducing the product to new markets where it will be perceived as novel
- Exporting can alleviate some of the problems encountered by seasonal products, enabling the producers of such products to sell year round

Licensing

Licensing is a contractual agreement between two companies whereby the owner of a brand name or patent (the licensor) gives a foreign company (the licensee) the right to use its brand name or patent in exchange for a fee or a royalty.

- The main benefit of licensing to licensors is that it offers an opportunity to further develop their brand or products
- Another benefit of licensing is that it provides the licensor with a way to capitalize upon—that is, to profit from—the expertise or some other capacity of the licensee, thus gaining revenue it would not have had if it had operated only in its domestic market
- A third benefit to the licensor is that frequently the licensee often must pay the licensor for startup assistance, for materials, and to obtain the licensor's consulting expertise
- Licensing also opens markets to the licensor to which it previously had no access

Joint Venture

A joint venture may be defined as a business enterprise in which two or more companies agree to undertake a new economic endeavor together. Each of the companies contributes equity to the new venture, and each of them shares in its revenues, expenses, and operation. The new venture can be a single project or a broader, continuing business relationship.

Among the benefits accruing to the partners in an international joint venture are:

- The individual companies can share their expertise, thus creating a more comprehensive approach to developing and selling the product
- The venture can provide entry into markets which have been closed to foreign companies
- Risks are shared by the participants, limiting the amount of risk a single entity might be exposed to
- Goods produced locally in foreign countries can get to their markets faster than imported goods
- By joining forces, the contributing entities are better able to compete with rival enterprises

Franchising

Franchising is a form of business organization in which an established firm which is selling an already established and profitable product or service (the franchisor) enters into a business agreement with another business which will operate under the franchisor's name (the franchisee) in a given market, usually for a fee.

- Franchising in global markets has some of the same benefits as those that accrue to franchisers within a national market: the ability to capitalize on a known name brand; marketing and management assistance from the franchisor; and a traditionally lower failure rate than independent startups
- But the global market offers a firm the chance to establish its presence across national borders, with the potential to vastly increase its customer base and, consequently, its profits

FDI

Foreign direct investment (FDI) refers to the practice of buying property and businesses incorporated in foreign countries.

- And the most common type of FDI is what is known as a foreign subsidiary, in which a domestic company (known as the parent company) directly owns a company in a foreign country (called the subsidiary)
- In an FDI, the parent company provides direct investment of buildings, machinery, and equipment in the subsidiary, in contrast to what is called a portfolio investment, which is often termed an indirect investment
- An FDI can take a number of different forms, from the outright purchase of a foreign firm to the construction of a production facility or participation in a joint venture or strategic alliance with a foreign entity
- The parent company gains new markets and marketing channels and often cheaper production facilities, in addition to the technical expertise and skills it gains from the subsidiary
- The subsidiary may receive, in addition to the capital invested by the parent company, new technologies and management skills, which can lead to its own economic expansion

Strategic Alliance

A strategic alliance is a form of partnership among two or more companies which seek to build a market advantage over their common competitors while retaining their identities as independent companies. Unlike a joint venture, however, a strategic alliance involves no equity stake or sharing of risks by the participants.

Among the benefits accruing to partners in a strategic alliance:

- These arrangements provide their participants with new access to markets, funding, distribution channels, manufacturing capability, and technical expertise
- Strategic alliances allow each individual participant to concentrate on those activities in which it has particular expertise
- The sharing of expenses and risk provides each participant with significantly lower exposure to catastrophic loss in the case of difficulties or failure

Developing Nation's Economic Forces

In working in developing nations, it is important to be aware of the extent to which these nations' per capita income will affect what might initially appear to be great business opportunities—the population there might not earn enough to purchase your goods or services.

Since there is no global currency, businesses must take into account the current exchange rate, which describes the value of a foreign nation's currency against one's own.

- A high value for the dollar means that it takes more of the local currency of a foreign nation to purchase American goods than would be the case if the dollar held a lower value
- Labor costs are directly affected by the exchange rate, causing fluctuations in the cost of production, which if properly managed can be a benefit, but if poorly managed can result in severe difficulties

Global Markets Sociology Forces

First, we may define the study of sociology as including the scientific examination of the cultures which have developed among a discrete and identifiable group of people, often circumscribed by a geographical area such as a country or a tribe, including such structures as values, beliefs, rules, and institutions.

- In seeking to conduct business operations in foreign countries or in cooperation with foreign cultures, it is crucial for businesses to be aware of these differences in culture in order to effectively maximize their business potential and avoid inadvertently behaving in a manner which might be considered insensitive or offensive to another culture
- Language is a very important consideration, as literal translations of common phrases can often translate into silly, nonsensical, or even offensive formulations in another language
- Religion is another one of the cultural factors which must be taken into consideration when doing business with a foreign country, and many examples can be found where even very enlightened companies have committed cultural gaffes which have proved injurious to their business operations in foreign countries

Environmental and Physical Forces

Developing nations present a particular challenge to businesses seeking to operate in the global marketplace.

- Communication systems, roads, and even such necessities as water and electricity are sometimes primitive, if not completely absent, in certain areas in many developing nations
- These types of difficulties are magnified when the business revolves around the production, distribution, and sale of food or food-related products, because to take excessive time to move these products from point of origin to point of sale will result in spoilage and loss
- And even if the technological resources are present in a foreign country, it may be the case that its system differs from the US system in ways that must be accounted for
- For example, many foreign countries use 220-volt electrical systems, requiring modifications to any device developed to run at 110 volts

Global Markets Difficulties

Since no global legal system exists, businesses have to contend with a myriad of federal, state, and local laws and regulations when attempting to do business in foreign markets.

- These laws and regulations run the gamut from child labor laws, copyright laws, product liability laws, and labor relations laws, to name just a few
- American businesses are also constrained by certain domestic legislation, such as the Foreign Corrupt Practices Act of 1978, which prohibits what it terms questionable or dubious payments—i.e., bribes—to foreign officials in order to establish business relationships
- In many foreign countries, these payments are an established way of doing business, and American firms are at a competitive disadvantage if they are forbidden to engage in them

Protective Tariffs

Protective tariffs are a tax or a duty is imposed upon imported goods and services, making them relatively more expensive to purchase than domestic products of the same type.

Revenue Tariffs

Revenue tariffs as in protective tariffs, a tax or a duty is imposed upon imported goods, the difference being that a revenue tariff is designed to raise money for the government.

Import Quotas

Import quotas is a form of protectionism works by limiting the quantity of a specified product or service or a specified category of products and services which are permitted to enter a nation in a specified span of time.

Embargos

Embargos are absolute bans upon the entry of a specified product or service or a specified category of products; also the absolute prohibition to do any business at all with a specified nation.

Nontariff Barriers

Nontariff barriers are not as specific as tariffs or quotas, nontariff barriers can include severe restrictions in the standards under which a product can be produced.

Trade Protectionism

Trade protectionism is the imposition of government regulation in the form of quotas or duties on imported goods and services for the purpose of protecting domestic business enterprises from foreign competition.

- Trade protectionism can limit the quantity of imported goods which are permitted to enter the country in a specified span of time
- Trade protectionism can consist of state subsidies to domestic businesses, in order to make domestic goods and services less expensive than those of their foreign competitors
- The most prevalent expression of trade protectionism comes in the form of tariffs on imports, which are fundamentally taxes which make these imports more expensive to purchase

Common Markets

Common markets (also known as trading blocs) are regional groups of countries that have joined together to promote duty-free trade and to facilitate the smooth movement of labor and financial resources among its member nations.

- Common markets magnify the strength of their individual member nations by joining together to eliminate tariffs within their boundaries and employing a common tariff on goods originating from outside their boundaries
- Common markets typically develop a legal framework under which trade among member nations is facilitated

EU

The European Union (EU) is an alliance of 25 member nations, whose total population now measures 455 million persons.

- The EU is now the world's second largest economic power, and uses this power in an attempt to compete with the other major economic powers such as the United States, China, and Japan
- The EU has adopted its own currency, called the euro, which has provided great economic benefit to its members by eliminating the need for (and the expense of) currency conversion

GATT

The General Agreement on Tariffs and Trade (GATT) was formed by the leaders of 23 nations in 1948, with the express goal of facilitating international trade by freezing and reducing tariff levels on a broad range of various commodities.

- Under GATT, member nations agreed to negotiate trade agreements in order to create a less restrictive flow of goods and services
- GATT was approved in the United States in 1994, and tariffs were lowered an average of 38 percent

WTO

The World Trade Organization (WTO) was established in the 1986 round of GATT negotiations.

- The WTO consists of 148 member nations and is headquartered in Geneva, Switzerland
- The objective of the WTO is to facilitate trade among member nations by administering global trade agreements and attempting to resolve disputes as they occur

Outsourcing

Outsourcing has come to be defined as the transfer of management to and/or the execution of a business enterprise in foreign countries.

- As unemployment in the United States has exceeded 10 percent, the term has now become virtually synonymous with the phenomenon of jobs which were once centered in the United States being performed by employees residing in foreign countries
- Perhaps the most visibly outsourced jobs are those in the tech industry
- Everyone in the United States has had the experience of trying to get customer service for their new piece of electronic gadgetry, only to be directed to a customer service representative in India

- Outsourcing is only expected to increase, especially with the emergence of China as a global economic superpower, reminding the United States of the importance of maintaining its edge through education and training

NAFTA

The North American Free Trade Agreement (NAFTA) was signed into law in 1994 among the United States, Canada, and Mexico.

- NAFTA was designed to facilitate free trade among its three member nations by phasing out tariffs and eliminating a variety of fees and other impediments to a freer flow of goods and services among its members
- Proponents of NAFTA point out that it has resulted in an increase of US exports to the other two member nations from $135 billion to $250 billion since the agreement was enacted
- They also argue that it strengthens the US economy by increasing sales and business for US companies
- Opponents of NAFTA have argued that it puts the United States at a competitive disadvantage through the loss of US jobs and capital; the US Department of Labor has estimated that the United States has lost 500,000 jobs since NAFTA was implemented

DSST Practice Test

1. Joe was tired of working for other people. He had an idea to start his own ice cream business and wanted to set it up where he alone would be responsible for the decisions and the rewards. In this case, his organization would be listed as...

a. limited partnership
b. general partnership
c. sole proprietorship
d. master limited partnership

2. Tom and Bill were good at fiberglass, spray painting, and boat making, so they wanted to develop a business that customized bass boats. They each had another job that was full time and also lacked the resources to fund their project with boats. A group of dentists knew both men and saw potential in their plan, so they offered to fund the start-up if Tom and Bill would handle operations. It started on weekends for both men but quickly expanded. In this case, the type of business ownership would be known as...

a. general partnership
b. limited partnership
c. master limited partnership
d. sole proprietorship

3. Jake's family made wonderful barbeque in their own backyard. They dug a pit, cut the white oak and hickory, and would even sit out all night on weekends while it cooked slowly over the smoke. Neighbors and family loved the products that came from Jake's pit. They even talked the family into starting a business around the concept. But Jake's family could not agree on any of the decisions, so they decided to appoint a board of directors who would operate as "officers" for the business, filed formal paperwork called "articles" and even held regular meetings with their board of directors. After the business started, Jake's group sold stock in it and actually paid a dividend. In this case, the type of business would be known as...

a. general partnership
b. limited partnership
c. master limited partnership
d. corporation

4. When it comes to corporations, creditors can seek recovery from...

a. shareholders
b. directors and officers
c. board of directors
d. assets of the corporation

5. Joe is in a partnership with his friend and neighbor, Tom. Both own and run a metal siding business in the area, but a recent housing drop has hindered their profits to the point where they are considering bankruptcy. They want to continue in business but struggle to repay their suppliers. Which of the following below would be the best option for them if they just need some time in order to make some changes and refocus their efforts?

a. Chapter 7
b. Chapter 11
c. Chapter 12
d. Chapter 13

6. Lucy has dreamed all her life for the day when she could run her own business. Friends tell her to consider a franchise since that would eliminate many of the risks facing new businesses. That sounds good to Lucy, but she has some hesitations. Which of the below are NOT a disadvantage when it comes to franchises?

a. being subject to corporate rules
b. large start-up costs
c. being forced out of business if other franchises in the chain fail
d. operating essentially as a sole proprietor even though you get help in management and marketing

7. Bowers' Plastics is a local firm that will be bought out by T-Rate Tennis Products, a multi-national corporation that is interested in the innovative approach that Bowers takes with their racquetball production. T-Rate specializes in a wide range of sports equipment; however, Bowers has only one specialization, and that's the way they produce racquetballs that retain their inner pressure longer than others on the market. What type of merger would be best for this?

a. vertical
b. horizontal
c. conglomerate
d. either "a" or "b"

8. Sole proprietorships face "unlimited liability." Which of the following is NOT true when it comes to that?

a. business losses become personal losses for the business owner
b. responsibility to liquidate assets to pay for business loss even if those assets include real estate, cars, or even funds from their own bank account
c. limits on personal losses if they exceed the owner's income
d. Only "a" and "c"

9. Shelia and Marcie are good at hair styling and decide to open their own beauty shop. It succeeds far beyond their expectations, so they move into a plan with the hope of franchising. Both draft the legal agreement that will form the basis of their contract. But Shelia worked in the medical field before this attempt, so she understands the risk that they could face when it comes to legal liability. So she suggests they set up their business with a "limited liability" clause in the formal agreement that they write. What does that mean?

a. Any partners are responsible for all debts and losses even beyond the value of their investment.
b. Any partners are not responsible for all debts and losses beyond the value of their investment.
c. Personal assets cannot be taken to compensate any creditors.
d. Both "b" and "c"

10. Foreign corporations are different from alien corporations in that...

a. both were incorporated in another country.
b. both are authorized to do business in an area where they were not incorporated.
c. both are within the US only.
d. only "a" and "b"

11. The *biggest* difference between open and closed corporations is that...

a. open corporations have their shares traded in the public market.
b. closed corporations have stock that is not available to the public.
c. closed corporations are closed to the public and have government backing.
d. both "a" and "b"
e. both "a" and "c"

12. What is <u>*not*</u> part of corporate bylaws?

a. location of the corporation and the date/location of corporate meetings
b. identification, duties of corporate officers, and how to select them
c. guidelines on how stock will be issued
d. individual staffing decisions and implementation of policy

13. What is <u>*not*</u> true of cooperatives?

a. They are owned by one individual and operated by the people who use the services.
b. They are both owned and operated by those who use the services.
c. Those who use the services of a cooperative can also work there.
d. One of the goals is to unite different groups like owners, managers, and consumers since the business provides for their common interests.

14. How is a "vision" different from an organization's "goal"?

a. Visions impart a sense of purpose, while a "goal" is the application of that.
b. Visions are broad statements that describe the organization's purpose and its future, but a goal is a specific strategy to achieve the organization's purpose.
c. Goals outline the purpose of an organization and a "vision" is the application of those individual plans.
d. Both "a" and "b".

15. What part of a business plan will address an organization's self concept, philosophy, long term survival, customer needs and social responsibility?

a. corporate vision
b. marketing plan
c. staffing policy
d. mission statement

16. What are important considerations in strategic planning?

a. identifying human and physical resources needed
b. deciding the products to see and the geographic areas to target
c. decisions relating to the customer base
d. staffing in production
e. all of the above
f. only "a" – "c"

17. What are important components in business "tactics"?

a. defining short term objectives to help achieve strategic plans for an organization
b. decision making by managers and workers at lower levels of an organization
c. finding resources and methods to reach specific objectives
d. only "a" and "b"
e. only "b" and "c"
f. all of the above

18. What is _not_ an important incentive for developing contingency plans in a business?

a. An organization may fail to achieve their goals.
b. High unemployment has increased the pool of eligible applicants.
c. Today's business environment can change fast.
d. Catastrophic events can affect a business in events like terrorism, identity theft and environmental disasters.

19. How is "organizational planning" different from "strategic plans"?

a. It's more broad-based with a look for trends that affect competitors.
b. Strategic planning is more related to a company's overall direction, while organizational planning targets the daily operations of specific departments and employees.
c. Organizational planning is a tool to measure an organization's stated goals.
d. Organizational planning targets standards and schedules in order to achieve business objectives.
e. Only "b", "c" and "d".
f. Only "b" and "d".

20. What is _not true_ when in a comparison between "problem solving" and "decision making" in a business setting?

a. Decision making is a fast process, while problem solving is a long and slow consideration of the components, implications, and outcome of your attempt.
b. Decision making is an extended analysis of a situation with possible solutions.
c. Problem solving confronts obstacles when fast resolution is needed, even when complete information is absent.
d. There is no formal strategy with problem solving since you use experience and ingenuity to develop a solution.

21. Issues relating to delegating, offering support, and morale building are components of...

a. human relations
b. conceptual skills
c. technical skills
d. production

22. Who are a company's "stakeholders," and why is it important to interact with them?

a. management, production, and company officers that could help develop policy and innovation
b. customers, employees, suppliers, and anyone in the company's area that might be affected by operations since any of those groups could affect the outcome of a business organization
c. hourly employees who helped to build and run a business since they hold the "stake" for the future of any business
d. creditors since they can restrict profits with their policies

23. How is leadership different from the process of management?

a. Leaders provide a vision for an organization, while managers provide stability in an organization.
b. Leaders help to motivate others to help achieve their vision, while managers work to maintain order.
c. Leaders attempt to influence an organization in a way to maximize its effectiveness, while managers promote corporate values.
d. Leaders help to promote corporate ethics, while managers help organizations maneuver major changes.

24. The type of leadership that is the most effective in an emergency or crisis would be...

a. autocratic, where the leader or manager makes decisions on their own
b. participative with the input from all sectors of stake holders
c. committee-centered
d. methodic and long-range

25. How has the concept of "empowerment" changed between managers and employees?

a. More managers are using an "autocratic" style since the economy worsened and the threat of terrorism increased.
b. More managers are using a process known as "directing," where they involve employees in the decision making process in order to increase participation in the organization and foster personal responsibility.
c. More managers are giving up total control to advance the objectives of the business and allow worker teams to develop policy relating to objectives, while the managers focus on strategic goals only.
d. There is less "empowerment" since the risk of job loss has increased.

26. The control process includes all of the following *except*...

a. established standards
b. zero tolerance for mistakes in education
b. monitored performance
c. communicated results
d. rewarded success and corrective action when needed

27. Which is the best statement to explain the process of marketing?

a. It is sales that could be defined as internal or external.
b. It is the communication or promotion of an object or service.
c. It is letting customers know that you can solve their problem with your product of service.
d. It is the activities, the group of institutions, and the processes for creating, communicating, delivering, and exchanging goods and services to customers and clients.

28. The four Ps of marketing is the focus on...

a. product, price, place (or location) and promotion.
b. practical value for the customer, priced lower than competition, packaging, and positive sales people.
c. predetermined strategy, pressure on competition, push in delivery, and pleasurable outcome for the customer.
d. none of the above

29. What is the final step in a marketing strategy?

a. generating publicity
b. providing follow-up services for customers to register their opinion of the product and give feedback
c. offering discounts, coupons, rebates and samples
d. encouraging viral recommendations

30. What are the four steps to market research?

a. First, collect data, analyze results, target customers, and present your solution.
b. Approach customers, compare existing items that are offered, package your item, and price to sell.
c. Consider your assets, compare the existing competition, consult customers, and offer a low cost alternative as a solution.
d. Consider the opportunity, collect data, interpret results, and offer a solution.

31. How is concept testing different from test marketing?

a. Both involve quantitative and qualitative methods to evaluate customer responses to a product or service, so there's no difference since they're part of the same process.
b. Concept testing uses customers to imagine the product in focus groups, while test marketing is a mass market approach with samples.
c. Concept testing is a presentation to customers in visual images or with the product to evaluate their likelihood of purchasing it, while test marketing is the process of actually trying the product out on a small group of representative customers.
d. Concept marketing involves customer participation in design and packaging, while test marketing is the use of samples and rebates to measure incremental difference in attraction.

32. Of the following, which is the best segmentation for market plans?

a. All segments which could lead to purchase of that product or service.
b. Geographic always, because that defines the boundaries of need.
c. Demographic first, because the shifting purchasing patterns follow age related interests.
d. Psychographic, because those groups will be more receptive to the product followed by distribution segmentation because delivery costs can eliminate all other considerations.

33. Which of the following is the best example of "niche" marketing?

a. McDonald's hamburgers, since it targets a large number of hungry people.
b. Model A Fords, since the assembly line process allowed the average American to purchase an automobile.
c. Dell computers, which provides a spectrum of computer-related products but also individually customizes for each and every individual consumer.
d. Coke, since local bottlers can take the same formula and apply it to their local water supply.

34. Compared with the mass marketing approach after WWII, how has the Internet affected marketing in recent years?

a. It allowed a lot of inexperienced business people to create their own web sites and offer products.
b. It helped to funnel large amounts of products and services to customers that were overlooked by traditional marketing.
c. It helped to streamline the marketing so that more customers participated in the mass marketing approach.
d. The emphasis shifted to customer needs and that opened niche markets that became accessible on the Internet.

35. What is the *best* reason to avoid global advertising campaigns?

a. The expense of reaching large numbers of potential customers can outweigh the benefits.
b. It takes extreme effort to translate the message into all the languages.
c. Cultural groups differ in their language patterns, habits, customs, and behavior so the risk of misunderstanding increases when the target area is expanded to a global scale.
d. Not every country will want your product or service since hostile areas could make marketing dangerous.

36. What is *missing* from the following "steps" in the selling process?

--Identify and qualify buyers who might be interested.

--Learn all you can about potential buyers.

--Make a good first impression.

--Link potential customers with a need for your product.

--Answer objections with a strategy that counters potential negative responses.

--Close the sale.

--Invite feedback to get the customer's impressions of the product, which can influence changes in strategy for the future.

a. Price adjustments are not mentioned.
b. Product design is not considered or adjusted.
c. Staffing is not addressed since sales have to include employees.
d. There is nothing missing since all the steps of the selling process are included.

37. Ralph wanted to start his own graphic design studio. He had an undergraduate degree in fine arts and worked in graphic designs for several years. However, his friend and partner, Ellen, told him to wait. She said it was a horrible time to start any business because, in her opinion, "we're in a major depression" since there's been a slight drop in the GDP (Gross Domestic Product), and their investment would probably sink like many other start-ups. How accurate was her advice when it comes to her assessment of the economy?

a. She was wrong since a depression is defined as a drop in the GDP of more than ten percent.
b. She is right since a depression is a slight drop in the GDP and consumer confidence falls.
c. She was wrong since there was only one period when GDP dropped to depression levels, and that was in the Great Depression from 1919 – 1933.
d. Both "a" and "c".

38. What is the *best answer* when you consider the balance between credit and the consideration of operating funds?

a. Operating funds are needed for payroll and making payments to lenders, so a business with too much credit that is tied up with customers can limit cash assets, make it harder to compete, and threaten the viability of a company.
b. Customers are the life blood of a business, so it's an advantage to offer credit to as many as possible since the interest made on that money will make up for the business loss of operating expenses.
c. They're not related, so this is not a potential problem.
d. Businesses exist to offer products and services, so there is no place for any credit offered to customers since all operating funds are needed to run the business.

39. What is an "unsecured loan," and why is this a risk in business?

a. The borrower offers no collateral so the loan is not backed by assets that can be taken in case the loan defaults.
b. The borrower gets a limited amount of funds that are not "secured" in time, so they can use that money whenever they want.
c. The borrower is unable to obtain a loan from a bank, so they take higher interest rates that are not "secured" to a fixed rate and can default on the lender.
d. The borrower is a business with an "unsecured" reputation for repayment, and that increases the risk for the lender.

40. What are some of the risks and rewards in issuing bonds when you're in business?

a. Bondholders are not owners in a company, so management maintains control of a company even though a bond increases the debt load on a company.
b. Interest paid to bondholders is tax deductible to the company issuing the bond, but the companies issuing bonds must pay interest to those who invest or they face legal action.
c. The value of the bond must be paid when the bond matures, or the company issuing the bond will risk the possibility of lower cash flow.
d. All the above.

41. How are commodities different from the Futures market?

a. A commodity is a physical substance like coffee, pork bellies, oil, wheat, or metals, but the Futures market focuses on the buying and selling of commodities, bonds or currency at a specific price on a specified future date.
b. Commodities are anything that can be "commodified" or consumed as a food, and the Futures market sells those.
c. Commodities are oil-related and not consumable, and the Futures market offers them for sale based on historic prices.
d. The term "commodities" refers to anything that consumers need, and the Futures market offers that for sale on Wall Street as the 2800 large companies on the New York Stock Exchange.

42. The Federal Reserve operates twelve Federal Reserve Banks with one central bank that buys and sells government bonds to increase or decrease the money supply.

That is known as...

a. reserve requirement
b. discount rate
c. advisory council
d. open-market operations

43. In accounting, what is the process of recording all transactions in two different locations to reduce the chance of error?

a. notes payable
b. statement of cash flows
c. accounts payable
d. double-entry bookkeeping

44. How can an economy be said to "recover" when unemployment is still above ten percent nationally?

a. An economic recovery occurs when an economy begins to grow. That can happen without an increase in employment.
b. An economic recovery happens when only employment increases since that is the indicator used to measure the viability of a market.
c. Inflation is the standard measure of the health in an economy. Employment does not affect recovery.
d. Either "b" or "c".

45. How could a weak US dollar best affect our business community?

a. Weak dollars encourage foreign investment overseas.
b. US goods become more expensive in foreign countries.
c. Foreign goods become cheaper in the US when the dollar is weak since their value is tied to US currency.
d. US goods become relatively cheaper in foreign countries while foreign goods become more expensive in the US

46. Joe's Hardware decides that they are going to cut out the competition when it comes to nails. They make a study of the competition and price their entire supply of nails lower than anyone in the area. That price remains fixed from then on and could be *best* described as...

a. skimming price strategy since the price of introducing the product tries to recover the costs of developing the product.
b. penetration strategy since the introduced product targets a large segment of the market by pricing the product low.
c. everyday low pricing since the price is set lower than competitors in order to siphon off their customers on an everyday basis.
d. psychological pricing since the item appears to be less expensive than it actually is to attract business.

47. Tom inherited a furniture manufacturing business from his father and wants to streamline his operations to remain competitive. What would be the best choice in logistics since he is in a major urban area with a lot of rail links near his factory?

a. Trucks would be the most cost effective approach since rail services can be hard to schedule on a regular basis and he would benefit from more flexibility.
b. Trains are the single largest form of transportation used in the US and can easily move large items cost effectively.
c. A combination of rail and truck could take advantage of both forms for cost cutting and the need for flexibility in case customer buying habits or gas prices change.
d. Shipping containers would be the most cost effective since that would protect his furniture from the weather.

48. Why is data mining an important application now for almost any business?

a. It uses sophisticated technological approaches to search for previously hidden patterns in data, and that could help in market research.
b. Technology can extract information from large amounts of data to find mistakes in possible mistakes in the production process.
c. The artificial intelligence and advanced statistical tools in the technology can find details that would be difficult for staff members who were looking through the same information if there was a possibility of fraud in bookkeeping.
d. All of the above.

49. What do employees value the most on a job--according to the research?

a. working conditions, like money and job security
b. job content, like a sense of achievement and recognition
c. the environment
d. shared values

50. Why is hiring someone who cheated in school a risk for businesses?

a. Students who cheat in school are more likely to be unethical on the job.
b. Students who are caught cheating are not very good at getting away with things.
c. Students who cheat show that they care more about the end than the means.
d. It isn't a risk. Students who cheat show that they are willing to do whatever it takes to succeed.

Answer Key and Explanations

1. C: In "a", limited partnership involves ownership with at least one other person, so this answer is wrong. With "b", a general partnership shares profits and liabilities, so this answer is wrong. In "c", a sole proprietorship is set up with the business owner making decisions and also getting the benefits or rewards, so this is the best answer. With "d", a master limited partnership is similar to a corporation, so there would not be one person taking ownership or making decisions.

2. B: When two or more people enter a business as owners, it's known as partnership. It can't be a general partnership because the investors funded the operation, so "a" is incorrect. A master limited partnership is similar to a corporation, so answer "c" is incorrect since only two men own the business. The answer "d" is incorrect since more than one man is involved in leading the company. The best answer would be "b", a limited partnership since there are several "limited" partners who invest in the business in addition to the general "partners" who operate it.

3. D: This can't be a general or limited partnership because a board of directors is acting as "officers" of the business. That makes "a", "b" and "c" wrong. The best answer is "d". There is no partnership effort in this effort. The board of directors makes decisions for Jake and his family when they barbeque.

4. D: In a corporation, the business is the owner, so the shareholders cannot be held responsible when creditors seek compensation over debts owed. That eliminates answer choices "a", "b" and "c". The only recourse that creditors have in seeking to collect on debts from a corporation would be to get it from the assets of the corporation.

5. B: In chapter 7, the debtor wants to be free from all repayment of debt. Their assets would then be sold and distributed to their creditors. This is not what Joe and Tom want since they just need more time in order to make some changes and continue in business, so answer choice "a" is wrong. In Chapter 11, the business is reorganized with a plan on how to repay the creditors. In addition, the plan addresses any changes or plans for the future. In that sense, answer choice "b" seems to be a good fit for Joe and Tom. Chapter 12 is for family farmers or fishermen, neither of which would apply to Joe and Tom, so answer choice "c" would not be right. Chapter 13 is to stop foreclosure actions in individual wage earners. This doesn't apply to Joe and Tom since their houses are not at risk, so answer choice "d" would not be right.

6. D: This is a judgment call since it involves opinions. Some business owners like to follow corporate rules. But this can get quite involved when it comes to the details that franchisees can face at all levels of their operation. There are exact rules about all stages of the business, and you can violate the contract by refusing to follow them as stated. That makes answer choice "a" more of a disadvantage. Traditionally, start up costs can be high for franchises. This can be a drain on new business owners at a time when they need capital. That makes answer choice "b" a disadvantage. Franchises are also at risk since their operations are standardized. Customers understand this and can make judgments about one outlet and generalize bad service or bad news about another in the same chain. That makes answer choice "c" a disadvantage. The best choice in this question would be "d" since it would be hard to see operating as a sole proprietor or help in management and marketing as a disadvantage.

7. A: In a vertical merger, two different businesses have different phases of a related business. They then join as one entity. This could be true of Bowers and T-Rate since they are both producing equipment for sports. In that sense, answer choice "a" would be a good fit. In a horizontal merger, two groups in the same industry decide to join and expand their products. This does not apply since Bowers only produces racquetballs and not other equipment for sports. Answer choice "b" or "d" would not be good. In a conglomerate merger, two firms that are unrelated decide to join forces and expand their product range. This would not apply in this case since they are both involved in equipment for sports. That eliminates answer choice "c".

8. C: Unlimited liability means there are no limits on the amount that you might have to pay if you are in a sole proprietorship. Both "a" and "b" represent the types of potential losses that you can face. This question is asking for the item that is NOT true when it comes to unlimited liability. Answer choice "c" is the best option since it doesn't matter how much income you make as a sole proprietorship. You're still responsible for any losses.

9. D: The word "limited" restricts a creditor. All partners are protected from damages that are larger than their investment. That eliminates answer choice "a". Both "b" and "c" are true, so answer choice "d" would be best since personal assets

cannot be taken by creditors, and the partners are not responsible for the amount of debt beyond the level of investment that each partner has in the business.

10. D: Both were incorporated in another state or country and are authorized to do business in another area. That could be another state from the area where they were incorporated. They can also be formed in another country from the US and be authorized to do business in the US

11. D: Open corporations have stock that is publicly traded. Closed corporations have stock that is not publicly traded. That makes both "a" and "b" correct. Answer choice "c" is incorrect because "quasi-public" corporations are the ones with government backing and are privately owned. The best answer choice in this question is "d".

12. D: Corporate bylaws are the rules that determine how a corporation will govern the organization. That includes location, meetings and officers. Individual staffing decisions are not part of corporate bylaws since that would be the application of those bylaws.

13. A: A cooperative is both owned and operated by people who make up different groups like the consumers, producers and workers, so it is not a sole proprietorship. Answer choices "b", "c" and "d" are all true of a cooperative. The answer choice that is not correct in this question is "a".

14. D: A vision both describes the organization's purpose and future as a broad statement while the goal is an application of that plan. Answer choice "c" is incorrect because a vision shows the direction that the organization wants to go in, and goals are the individual plans to accomplish that.

15. D: A "corporate vision" is the broad direction that an organization would like to go in. Market plans address sales, so answer choice "b" is incorrect. A "staffing policy" relates to employees only. A mission statement sets up an organization's fundamental purpose in concrete terms, so answer choice "d" would be the best choice.

16. F: The answer is "f" since staffing production would be more of a short term objective and not relating to the larger goals that are needed in strategic planning. In strategic planning, the need is for focus on major decisions relating to the fundamentals of business.

17. F: All of these are important components in business tactics since they deal with short-term objectives relating to strategic plans. Tactics are plans that target objectives. These are individual goals that the business develops ***after*** they set up their strategic plans. Tactics are based on strategic plans.

18. B: Contingency plans are the considerations that help organizations to confront the unexpected. Although an increased applicant pool can take a business off guard, the incentive for developing this type of planning is the unexpected problems with a larger impact—like terrorism, organization failure, or environmental disasters.

19. E: Organizational plans target objectives within the company like daily operations, specific departments, standards, and schedules. Strategic planning looks at the trends and broad issues that can affect a business.

20. A: Decision making is a slow process that takes in variables and works toward a conclusion. Problem solving can be a fast attempt that blends experience and ingenuity to develop a remedy. Decision making is more of a mental process with analysis and information. Problem solving is an application that targets a specific need.

21. A: Technical skills relate to specific disciplines like computer programming or design. Conceptual skills apply to planning, organizing, decision making and problem analysis. Production is the process of making an object. The best answer for this question is "a" since part of human relations applies to leading, delegating, supporting, and building morale among people.

22. B: Stakeholders are anyone affected by the business. They're important because the future and profit of any business can depend on the interaction that employees have with all of those affected. This is a major effort in the business world now as more organizations seek a competitive advantage and that often requires help from anyone related to a business.

23. A: Leaders provide vision, motivate others, influence organizations to embrace change, and promote ethics with corporate values. Managers are more interested in maintaining order and stability. The biggest difference is in their approach to change and innovation. Leaders are risk takers who try to inspire the best efforts and fair treatment in their organizations. Managers are more interested in control. That's why leaders are hard to find.

24. A: This is a judgment call. But in a crisis there may not be time to get information from stake holders or committees. There also may not be time to consider all the long term implications. It's always best to consider everyone involved in a decision but that may not be practical in a crisis. That's why "a" would be the best answer.

25. B: As workers are given more participation in the organization, the belief is that they will put forth greater effort and willingly accept more responsibility. To "empower" means to share in the decision making.

26. B: The control process is an organizational approach to increase worker performance. That would be difficult if an organization expected new workers to meet the same standards as experienced staff members. There has to be consideration for those who are learning new skills. All the other answer choices are correct when it comes to the control process. Each is a step to increase worker participation in business objectives.

27. D: Marketing involves sales, communication and promotion. But the best definition would have to include all elements including creating, delivering and exchanging a product or service with the process of selling it.

28. A: First, it has to be a product that the customer needs, priced to attract customers, placed in a target area and promoted to motivate customers. It helps to have practical value as in answer choice "a", but that doesn't apply to all marketing. Packaging, pleasurable outcomes and positive sales people can also help, but the best answer to explain the Four Ps in marketing is "a".

29. B: A marketing strategy includes all the activities used to promote a product and encourage sales. All of the answer choices are part of the marketing process. It helps to generate publicity, offer discounts and encourage awareness. But this question asked for the "final" step. That would have to include customer feedback to see if the marketing was effective.

30. D: Books have been written about this subject and there are differences of opinion. But market research has to start with a careful analysis of the need. There has to be data collection relating to that item or service. That will lead to a process of organizing and interpreting the results and, in turn, a targeted solution. Market research is a process with sequential steps.

31. C: Concept testing evaluates customer appeal and involves both quantitative and qualitative methods to measure those responses. The focus is on the appeal of a suggested product. In test marketing, a representative group of potential consumers is studied with the product to measure personal satisfaction and deficiencies relating to that product.

32. A: The answer is "a" because all of the other choices can be useful if they can help in isolation or in combination to sell the product. The best segmentation in marketing is a combination approach that pulls all the factors into consideration. The targeted outcome is a sale.

33. C: The answer is "c" since niche marketing is a process of targeting small segments or groups. Individualized approaches with business make it easy to focus on the needs of people that differ from large groups. A niche is a small segment of a larger market.

34. D: After WWII, there was an increased need for goods and services, and the marketing concept era began. That led to more emphasis on customer needs. The Internet helped business groups to target those markets and streamline their approaches.

35. C: Cultures differ widely when it comes to habits with products, services, and even their understanding of advertising. Although each of the answers in this question was technically correct, the ***best*** answer for the reason to avoid global marketing is the differences among cultures since any attempt would be a challenge to gain understanding.

36. D: The selling process is a series of steps that considers potential customers, investigates their personal need, and offers your product or service as a solution. One of the most important steps is the follow-up after a sale to gather information that helps in making adjustments for later sales.

37. D: An economic depression is a drop in the GDP of more than ten percent, so answer choice "a" is right. But answer choice "c" is also right since there has only been one period in our national history to fit that definition. That makes answer choice "d" the best option since it includes both.

38. A: It's true that customers are the life blood of a business. It's also true that businesses can profit from consumer debt. But that also limits operating funds that can be needed to run the business. In this question, the best answer is a balance that considers all the factors. That makes answer choice "a" the best option.

39. A: Unsecured loans are given with no collateral, which means the lender's investment can be lost if the loan defaults since there's no collateral that can be recovered.

40. D: Although there are benefits to the issuing of bonds when companies need to raise capital, there are also risks since they increase their debt load and are now responsible to the bond owners.

41. A: Commodities are physical substances that are bought and sold. That includes oil, wheat and metals. But the Futures market offers traders a pledge to conduct transactions at a future date. So if you agree to buy a shipment of oil at $40, you get that price at the agreed upon date regardless of changes in the market.

42. D: The "reserve" is the amount of money and liquid assets that Federal Reserve System member banks must keep as a percentage of their checking and savings accounts. The discount rate is the interest rate charged by the Fed when member banks want to borrow money from the Federal Reserve.

43. D: Notes payable is a loan from a bank or other source with a promise to repay by a specific date. Statements of cash flow summarize the money coming into or flowing out of the company like cash receipts and cash payments. Accounts payable are current liabilities owed for merchandise or services.

44. A: An economic recovery starts when the economy begins to grow. You can have that without an increase in employment. That makes answer choice "a" correct.

45. D: A lower value on US dollars means that fewer goods and services can be purchased with it. That makes US goods cheaper overseas and foreign goods more expensive in the US Answer choice "a" has some truth to it since foreign investors would be more likely to invest overseas when the dollar weakens. But the question asks how a weak dollar affects <u>*our*</u> business community. It can be argued that less foreign investment could hurt our economy, which is true. But the better answer is choice "d" since our goods would then become more attractive to foreign buyers when the dollar is weak. That would increase sales. Answer choices "c" is incorrect because weaker dollars would make foreign goods more expensive in this country.

46. C: The answer is "c" because that's the price and it's set to undercut competitors on a regular basis. All the other items in this answer are correctly defined but don't apply to Joe's example.

47. C: The best answer is "c" since a combination approach would take advantage of both forms. Freight rates are cheaper on rail but trucks add flexibility, so both could help.

48. D: Data mining has many uses for any business. This is an area that will only grow in application and opportunity.

49. B: Psychologist Frederick Herzberg studied this and concluded that most people assume the biggest motivators on the job are salary-related (which is important) but Herzberg's research shows the need for self-esteem at the workplace. That doesn't cost much to provide. Just treat employees with respect and point out their successes.

50. A: Students who cheat in school will take those behavior habits into the work setting. This is behind the need for more ethical understanding in the business world.

How to Overcome Test Anxiety

Just the thought of taking a test is enough to make most people a little nervous. A test is an important event that can have a long-term impact on your future, so it's important to take it seriously and it's natural to feel anxious about performing well. But just because anxiety is normal, that doesn't mean that it's helpful in test taking, or that you should simply accept it as part of your life. Anxiety can have a variety of effects. These effects can be mild, like making you feel slightly nervous, or severe, like blocking your ability to focus or remember even a simple detail.

If you experience test anxiety—whether severe or mild—it's important to know how to beat it. To discover this, first you need to understand what causes test anxiety.

Causes of Test Anxiety

While we often think of anxiety as an uncontrollable emotional state, it can actually be caused by simple, practical things. One of the most common causes of test anxiety is that a person does not feel adequately prepared for their test. This feeling can be the result of many different issues such as poor study habits or lack of organization, but the most common culprit is time management. Starting to study too late, failing to organize your study time to cover all of the material, or being distracted while you study will mean that you're not well prepared for the test. This may lead to cramming the night before, which will cause you to be physically and mentally exhausted for the test. Poor time management also contributes to feelings of stress, fear, and hopelessness as you realize you are not well prepared but don't know what to do about it.

Other times, test anxiety is not related to your preparation for the test but comes from unresolved fear. This may be a past failure on a test, or poor performance on tests in general. It may come from comparing yourself to others who seem to be performing better or from the stress of living up to expectations. Anxiety may be driven by fears of the future—how failure on this test would affect your educational and career goals. These fears are often completely irrational, but they can still negatively impact your test performance.

Elements of Test Anxiety

As mentioned earlier, test anxiety is considered to be an emotional state, but it has physical and mental components as well. Sometimes you may not even realize that you are suffering from test anxiety until you notice the physical symptoms. These can include trembling hands, rapid heartbeat, sweating, nausea, and tense muscles. Extreme anxiety may lead to fainting or vomiting. Obviously, any of these symptoms can have a negative impact on testing. It is important to recognize them as soon as they begin to occur so that you can address the problem before it damages your performance.

The mental components of test anxiety include trouble focusing and inability to remember learned information. During a test, your mind is on high alert, which can help you recall information and stay focused for an extended period of time. However, anxiety interferes with your mind's natural processes, causing you to blank out, even on the questions you know well. The strain of testing during anxiety makes it difficult to stay focused, especially on a test that may take several hours. Extreme anxiety can take a huge mental toll, making it difficult not only to recall test information but even to understand the test questions or pull your thoughts together.

Effects of Test Anxiety

Test anxiety is like a disease—if left untreated, it will get progressively worse. Anxiety leads to poor performance, and this reinforces the feelings of fear and failure, which in turn lead to poor performances on subsequent tests. It can grow from a mild nervousness to a crippling condition. If allowed to progress, test anxiety can have a big impact on your schooling, and consequently on your future.

Test anxiety can spread to other parts of your life. Anxiety on tests can become anxiety in any stressful situation, and blanking on a test can turn into panicking in a job situation. But fortunately, you don't have to let anxiety rule your testing and determine your grades. There are a number of relatively simple steps you can take to move past anxiety and function normally on a test and in the rest of life.

Physical Steps for Beating Test Anxiety

While test anxiety is a serious problem, the good news is that it can be overcome. It doesn't have to control your ability to think and remember information. While it may take time, you can begin taking steps today to beat anxiety.

Just as your first hint that you may be struggling with anxiety comes from the physical symptoms, the first step to treating it is also physical. Rest is crucial for having a clear, strong mind. If you are tired, it is much easier to give in to anxiety. But if you establish good sleep habits, your body and mind will be ready to perform optimally, without the strain of exhaustion. Additionally, sleeping well helps you to retain information better, so you're more likely to recall the answers when you see the test questions.

Getting good sleep means more than going to bed on time. It's important to allow your brain time to relax. Take study breaks from time to time so it doesn't get overworked, and don't study right before bed. Take time to rest your mind before trying to rest your body, or you may find it difficult to fall asleep.

Along with sleep, other aspects of physical health are important in preparing for a test. Good nutrition is vital for good brain function. Sugary foods and drinks may give a burst of energy but this burst is followed by a crash, both physically and emotionally. Instead, fuel your body with protein and vitamin-rich foods.

Also, drink plenty of water. Dehydration can lead to headaches and exhaustion, especially if your brain is already under stress from the rigors of the test. Particularly if your test is a long one, drink water during the breaks. And if possible, take an energy-boosting snack to eat between sections.

Along with sleep and diet, a third important part of physical health is exercise. Maintaining a steady workout schedule is helpful, but even taking 5-minute study breaks to walk can help get your blood pumping faster and clear your head. Exercise also releases endorphins, which contribute to a positive feeling and can help combat test anxiety.

When you nurture your physical health, you are also contributing to your mental health. If your body is healthy, your mind is much more likely to be healthy as well. So take time to rest, nourish your body with healthy food and water, and get moving as much as possible. Taking these physical steps will make you stronger and more able to take the mental steps necessary to overcome test anxiety.

Mental Steps for Beating Test Anxiety

Working on the mental side of test anxiety can be more challenging, but as with the physical side, there are clear steps you can take to overcome it. As mentioned earlier, test anxiety often stems from lack of preparation, so the obvious solution is to prepare for the test. Effective studying may be the most important weapon you have for beating test anxiety, but you can and should employ several other mental tools to combat fear.

First, boost your confidence by reminding yourself of past success—tests or projects that you aced. If you're putting as much effort into preparing for this test as you did for those, there's no reason you should expect to fail here. Work hard to prepare; then trust your preparation.

Second, surround yourself with encouraging people. It can be helpful to find a study group, but be sure that the people you're around will encourage a positive attitude. If you spend time with others who are anxious or cynical, this will only contribute to your own anxiety. Look for others who are motivated to study hard from a desire to succeed, not from a fear of failure.

Third, reward yourself. A test is physically and mentally tiring, even without anxiety, and it can be helpful to have something to look forward to. Plan an activity following the test, regardless of the outcome, such as going to a movie or getting ice cream.

When you are taking the test, if you find yourself beginning to feel anxious, remind yourself that you know the material. Visualize successfully completing the test. Then take a few deep, relaxing breaths and return to it. Work through the questions carefully but with confidence, knowing that you are capable of succeeding.

Developing a healthy mental approach to test taking will also aid in other areas of life. Test anxiety affects more than just the actual test—it can be damaging to your mental health and even contribute to depression. It's important to beat test anxiety before it becomes a problem for more than testing.

Study Strategy

Being prepared for the test is necessary to combat anxiety, but what does being prepared look like? You may study for hours on end and still not feel prepared. What you need is a strategy for test prep. The next few pages outline our recommended steps to help you plan out and conquer the challenge of preparation.

Step 1: Scope Out the Test

Learn everything you can about the format (multiple choice, essay, etc.) and what will be on the test. Gather any study materials, course outlines, or sample exams that may be available. Not only will this help you to prepare, but knowing what to expect can help to alleviate test anxiety.

Step 2: Map Out the Material

Look through the textbook or study guide and make note of how many chapters or sections it has. Then divide these over the time you have. For example, if a book has 15 chapters and you have five days to study, you need to cover three chapters each day. Even better, if you have the time, leave an extra day at the end for overall review after you have gone through the material in depth.

If time is limited, you may need to prioritize the material. Look through it and make note of which sections you think you already have a good grasp on, and which need review. While you are studying, skim quickly through the familiar sections and take more time on the challenging parts.

Write out your plan so you don't get lost as you go. Having a written plan also helps you feel more in control of the study, so anxiety is less likely to arise from feeling overwhelmed at the amount to cover.

Step 3: Gather Your Tools

Decide what study method works best for you. Do you prefer to highlight in the book as you study and then go back over the highlighted portions? Or do you type out notes of the important information? Or is it helpful to make flashcards that you can carry with you? Assemble the pens, index cards, highlighters, post-it notes, and any other materials you may need so you won't be distracted by getting up to find things while you study.

If you're having a hard time retaining the information or organizing your notes, experiment with different methods. For example, try color-coding by subject with colored pens, highlighters, or post-it notes. If you learn better by hearing, try recording yourself reading your notes so you can listen while in the car, working out, or simply sitting at your desk. Ask a friend to quiz you from your flashcards, or try teaching someone the material to solidify it in your mind.

Step 4: Create Your Environment

It's important to avoid distractions while you study. This includes both the obvious distractions like visitors and the subtle distractions like an uncomfortable chair (or a too-comfortable couch that makes you want to fall asleep). Set up the best study environment possible: good lighting and a comfortable work area. If background music helps you focus, you may want to turn it on, but otherwise keep the room quiet. If you are using a computer to take notes, be sure you don't have any other windows open, especially applications like social media, games, or anything else that could distract you. Silence your phone and turn off notifications. Be sure to keep water close by so you stay hydrated while you study (but avoid unhealthy drinks and snacks).

Also, take into account the best time of day to study. Are you freshest first thing in the morning? Try to set aside some time then to work through the material. Is your mind clearer in the afternoon or evening? Schedule your study session then. Another method is to study at the same time of day that you will take the test, so that your brain gets used to working on the material at that time and will be ready to focus at test time.

Step 5: Study!

Once you have done all the study preparation, it's time to settle into the actual studying. Sit down, take a few moments to settle your mind so you can focus, and begin to follow your study plan. Don't give in to distractions or let yourself procrastinate. This is your time to prepare so you'll be ready to fearlessly approach the test. Make the most of the time and stay focused.

Of course, you don't want to burn out. If you study too long you may find that you're not retaining the information very well. Take regular study breaks. For example, taking five minutes out of every hour to walk briskly, breathing deeply and swinging your arms, can help your mind stay fresh.

As you get to the end of each chapter or section, it's a good idea to do a quick review. Remind yourself of what you learned and work on any difficult parts. When you feel that you've mastered the material, move on to the next part. At the end of your study session, briefly skim through your notes again.

But while review is helpful, cramming last minute is NOT. If at all possible, work ahead so that you won't need to fit all your study into the last day. Cramming overloads your brain with more information than it can process and retain, and your tired mind may struggle to recall even previously learned information when it is overwhelmed with last-minute study. Also, the urgent nature of cramming and the stress placed on your brain contribute to anxiety. You'll be more likely to go to the test feeling unprepared and having trouble thinking clearly.

So don't cram, and don't stay up late before the test, even just to review your notes at a leisurely pace. Your brain needs rest more than it needs to go over the information again. In fact, plan to finish your studies by noon or early afternoon the day before the test. Give your brain the rest of the day to relax or focus on other things, and get a good night's sleep. Then you will be fresh for the test and better able to recall what you've studied.

Step 6: Take a Practice Test

Many courses offer sample tests, either online or in the study materials. This is an excellent resource to check whether you have mastered the material, as well as to prepare for the test format and environment.

Check the test format ahead of time: the number of questions, the type (multiple choice, free response, etc.), and the time limit. Then create a plan for working through them. For example, if you have 30 minutes to take a 60-question test, your limit is 30 seconds per question. Spend less time on the questions you know well so that you can take more time on the difficult ones.

If you have time to take several practice tests, take the first one open book, with no time limit. Work through the questions at your own pace and make sure you fully understand them. Gradually work up to taking a test under test conditions: sit at a desk with all study materials put away and set a timer. Pace yourself to make sure you finish the test with time to spare and go back to check your answers if you have time.

After each test, check your answers. On the questions you missed, be sure you understand why you missed them. Did you misread the question (tests can use tricky wording)? Did you forget the information? Or was it something you hadn't learned? Go back and study any shaky areas that the practice tests reveal.

Taking these tests not only helps with your grade, but also aids in combating test anxiety. If you're already used to the test conditions, you're less likely to worry about it, and working through tests until you're scoring well gives you a confidence boost. Go through the practice tests until you feel comfortable, and then you can go into the test knowing that you're ready for it.

Test Tips

On test day, you should be confident, knowing that you've prepared well and are ready to answer the questions. But aside from preparation, there are several test day strategies you can employ to maximize your performance.

First, as stated before, get a good night's sleep the night before the test (and for several nights before that, if possible). Go into the test with a fresh, alert mind rather than staying up late to study.

Try not to change too much about your normal routine on the day of the test. It's important to eat a nutritious breakfast, but if you normally don't eat breakfast at all, consider eating just a protein bar. If you're a coffee drinker, go ahead and have your normal coffee. Just make sure you time it so that the caffeine doesn't wear off right in the middle of your test. Avoid sugary beverages, and drink enough water to stay hydrated but not so much that you need a restroom break 10 minutes into the test. If your test isn't first thing in the morning, consider going for a walk or doing a light workout before the test to get your blood flowing.

Allow yourself enough time to get ready, and leave for the test with plenty of time to spare so you won't have the anxiety of scrambling to arrive in time. Another reason to be early is to select a good seat. It's helpful to sit away from doors and windows, which can be distracting. Find a good seat, get out your supplies, and settle your mind before the test begins.

When the test begins, start by going over the instructions carefully, even if you already know what to expect. Make sure you avoid any careless mistakes by following the directions.

Then begin working through the questions, pacing yourself as you've practiced. If you're not sure on an answer, don't spend too much time on it, and don't let it shake your confidence. Either skip it and come back later, or eliminate as many wrong answers as possible and guess among the remaining ones. Don't dwell on these questions as you continue—put them out of your mind and focus on what lies ahead.

Be sure to read all of the answer choices, even if you're sure the first one is the right answer. Sometimes you'll find a better one if you keep reading. But don't second-guess yourself if you do immediately know the answer. Your gut instinct is usually right. Don't let test anxiety rob you of the information you know.

If you have time at the end of the test (and if the test format allows), go back and review your answers. Be cautious about changing any, since your first instinct tends to be correct, but make sure you didn't misread any of the questions or accidentally mark the wrong answer choice. Look over any you skipped and make an educated guess.

At the end, leave the test feeling confident. You've done your best, so don't waste time worrying about your performance or wishing you could change anything. Instead, celebrate the successful completion of this test. And finally, use this test to learn how to deal with anxiety even better next time.

Review Video: Test Anxiety
Visit mometrix.com/academy and enter code: 100340

Important Qualification

Not all anxiety is created equal. If your test anxiety is causing major issues in your life beyond the classroom or testing center, or if you are experiencing troubling physical symptoms related to your anxiety, it may be a sign of a serious physiological or psychological condition. If this sounds like your situation, we strongly encourage you to seek professional help.

Online Resources

Due to our efforts to try to keep this book to a manageable length, we've created a link that will give you access to all of your online resources:

mometrix.com/resources719/dsstintrobus

It's Your Moment, Let's Celebrate It!

Share your story @mometrixtestpreparation